LAUREN
HOLMES

BIOMAXED

Dedicated to those who achieve sustained self-love through the pure creative self-expression of their essence in serial shared creations

CONTENTS

1

THE BIOLOGICALLY MAXIMIZED LIFE

"Two of the most important days in your life are the day you were born and the day you find out why."   Mark Twain

---

Prepare to transcend! Human potential is not limited to our DNA. It is actually based on how well you exploit the biological infrastructure all around us with which we have co-evolved to operate. A complex "machinery" has evolved to maximize all living systems for survival – including us. With a formulaic change to our modus operandi, our systems, circuits, and mechanisms are suddenly extended by counterparts in this maximizing machinery. From this simple change, we experience an exponential explosion in our potential.

New spontaneous-knowledge faculties. A more extensive information database beyond what you've collected from your five senses. A new directional guidance system which will have you moving in the ideal direction for your system and your goals yet entirely consistent with the direction of humanity and the world. There is no greater strategic advantage for product developers or world builders.

Altered and expanded consciousnesses will incite new states of knowing, information access, and uncanny predictive powers to enhance your decision-making and goal achievement. New mechanisms for creativity, innovation and invention will make even non-creatives creative world changers.

You will thrill to accelerated achievement through the dramatic increase of coincidences, breakthroughs, and epiphanies in your life. One coincidence can bypass hundreds of steps to catapult you to your goal. One breakthrough can be life-changing and even world-changing. Imagine a lifetime of serial breakthroughs. What could you accomplish? What could your legacy be?

And what could you achieve with improvements to your cognitive skills: better abstract thinking, conceptual thinking, big-picture thinking, systems thinking, strategic thinking, mental agility, adaptivity, pattern recognition, trend perception, environmental scanning, problem re-framing, and ambiguity resolution, for example.

It is interesting that these are the very meta-skills we look for in our executives. Since few courses are effective in developing these cognitive strengths, the proposed formulaic change in modus operandi may be a new creator of executive talent.

Imagine the joy of a career driven by "paid play, " "paid growth," and "paid learning," or where discipline and the need to push yourself are replaced by the pull of addictive drives and emotional highs. Now you can accomplish more than you ever thought yourself capable by being paid to never work again. This is the aim of the biologically maximized career.

These *BioMaxed* articles will introduce you to your true *internally-externally-sourced potential*. Learn what is possible when you extend your capabilities with those of this maximizing machinery and all of the living systems it governs. The whole will exceed the sum of the parts. Yet there will be more.

Accelerated growth, ever increasing functionality upgrades, and the emergence of evolved states will continually increase your level of peak performance. What you could not accomplish yesterday could be effortless today. Internal potential may have limits. External potential, however, is infinite.

BioMaxed plays a pivotal role in the development of my science. As you may have gathered, all of my books – fiction and nonfiction – explore the new level of human potential possible through a partnership with the biological infrastructure of which we are a part and with which we have co-evolved to operate.

Peak Evolution: Beyond Peak Performance and Peak Experience (2001, 2010) is the primer where I first began defining methods for exploiting nature's maximizing machinery and describing what happens over time as one complies with its direction and wields its massive resources.

The peak evolution strategies arose from experimenting with and researching what I had learned from interviewing 300 accomplished change executives from global multinationals in a compressed period of time. What I observed was then colored by my degree in biological anthropology.

BioMaxed (2019) is a collection of articles I wrote in 2013 and 2014. They helped me to examine some of the latest scientific findings and my more recent conclusions, methods, and applications that had emerged to refine the 2001 peak evolution science.

For those who have read the primer, you will see a more powerful and profound methodology more simply stated from a more expansive perspective. It is an unfortunate challenge

BioMaxed was an important transition for me that you can observe in the progression of the articles. I grew from upgrading the science to applying it to various fields – to provide guidance on how people might apply the science to achieve specific goals.

The Encore: A Transformational Thriller (2018) was an exciting opportunity to reveal my more advanced understanding of the internal-external partnership in action through helping *fictional* characters to become heroic worldbuilders to save a planet. They comprise the supporting cast of the book's real main character, transformation.

Savanting is what I now call the methodology for exploiting the internal-external partnership. *Savanting: Outperforming your Potential* (2019) is a chance to see the same partnership in action in the lives of *real* people this time. First, the savants for which savanting is named are introduced. I then try to retrofit my science onto the careers of accomplished individuals whose lives are well known – entrepreneurial CEOs Bill Gates, Steve Jobs, Jeff Bezos, Mark Zuckerberg, and media mogul, Oprah.

Immediately after writing the *BioMaxed* articles, I tried to push the envelope on the science in an early draft of *Savanting*. It was originally to be a significantly more advanced sequel to *Peak Evolution*.

However, everything in my world and inside of me blocked my progress. The maximizing machinery was against it. After I had written all of the people analyses which you will still find in *Savanting*, ideas for *The Encore* plot just took over and were too compelling to resist.

My goal for *Savanting* had been to demonstrate how the maximizing machinery operates so that people would get to know their potential partner. However, the maximizing machinery seemed to favor my achieving this goal through fictional characters.

I feel I was only a co-author of *The Encore* thriller with its incredibly challenging mandate: the twists and turns of a thriller plot; the resolution of a very real threat to the survival of Earth and humanity; the transformational promise; the application of an extremely complex science which is not mainstream; as well as the development of characters which I loved and hoped readers would too.

With the magic of a plethora of incredible coincidences, breakthroughs, epiphanies, and creative inspirations, plus directional guidance, I feel this book was definitely co-authored by the maximizing machinery – or what I call in *The Encore*, "the bioflow" – which seemed to decide on the best story for me and for humanity. It was a magical experience which I never saw coming. I cannot wait for the next.

The Encore is the first of what I hope will become a transformational series of novels showing many different applications of the science from which practitioners may learn how to exploit the internal-external partnership. But more than this, I hope the series will help people to experience the evolved states that will emerge as one spends more time living fully integrated into the maximizing bio-infrastructure.

I am not only talking about the commonly acknowledged evolved states such as unity consciousness or those reverent states esteemed by religious or spiritual disciplines. The essence of nature and the universe is endless creativity, adaptivity and advance. If you fully integrate into the evolutionary flow, this essence will emerge in you. The dedication I wrote for this book is an example of just such an evolved state I wish for everyone:

Dedicated to those who achieve sustained self-love through the pure creative self-expression of their essence in serial shared creations.

2

OVERVIEW OF THE *BIOMAXED* ARTICLES

THE BIOLOGICALLY MAXIMIZED CAREER

The Ultimate Career Strategy – What do the founders of Amazon, Microsoft, Apple, Google and Facebook teach us?

Intrinsically rewarding and biologically maximized careers. Could this career strategy provide a new framework from which to coach, parent, and lead? Could it redefine talent attraction, retention, development, and succession? Is this a new route to spontaneous leadership creation from the inside? Is this a way to maximize the human resources of the world to make their greatest contribution to the advance of humanity?

The Secret Career Strategy of the World's Most Successful Executives

Find out the career strategy shared by super-achievers Bill Gates (Microsoft co-founder), Steve Jobs and Steve Wozniak (Apple co-founders), Mark Zuckerberg (Facebook founder), Larry Page and Sergey Brin (Google co-founders), and Jeff Bezos (Amazon founder) and how you can use it to attain their tangible and intangible career rewards.

The New Career Maximums – Part One: Are you settling for too little?

Learn how to achieve beyond your potential with a biologically maximized career. Learn how serial breakthroughs and flashes of genius are accessible to all for life-changing and world-changing careers.

The New Career Maximums – Part Two: Are you settling for too little?

Learn how to sustain serial breakthroughs, serial growth, serial frontiering™, and serial flow states as a way of life to achieve at the level of the iconic founders of Microsoft, Apple, Facebook, Google, and Amazon.

Sourcing your Savant: Hyper-Focus your Career on your Genius

An unprecedented approach lets you discover your personal formula for your biologically maximized career. An inventory of twelve patterns of events in your past will incredibly all point you in the same direction. Capitalize on this past predictability for future success.

Reset to your Maximum to outperform your potential

Our cultures have taught us to be separate biological entities. Our potential then would be limited to what is within us. Yet, we have been born into a massive biological machinery. When we learn to drive that machinery and all of the systems it orchestrates, we will begin to know true human potential. This exercise will put you into that powerful driver's seat.

BIOLOGICALLY MAXIMIZED WORK AND ACHIEVEMENT

Savanting – Outperforming your Potential

The bar has been raised on human potential. Don't be left behind! Accelerate and amplify your achievements by increasing the quantity and quality of the information leaps that you experience. Learn how to generate coincidences, breakthroughs, epiphanies, flashes of genius, and creative inspirations to catapult you to your goals.

Frontiering is the new Leadership. The person who can frontier will always be the leader.

There is no leadership without frontiering™ in a world of accelerating change. Today, leadership is defined by the degree of frontiering™. Leaders lead people into unknown territory or bring the unknown into existence. The person with mastery of the unknown will always be the leader.

Managers manage what exists. Leaders bring the new into existence. Leaders penetrate new territories. They frontier. They create. They change reality. Leadership is not required if you are standing still. The person with the expertise for penetrating the unknown will always be the leader. Learn how to release your frontiering™ finesse.

NEW EXECUTIVE FUNCTIONALITY
AND EVOLVED STATES

Enhanced functionality will include serial breakthroughs, flashes of genius, sudden knowledge, sudden creativity, performance beyond potential, and a facility for innovation and scaling unknown frontiers. It will include much of the advanced functionality normally selected for leading large multinationals.

Many executive meta-skills emerge from a single paradigm shift to partnering with the massive biological adaptation machinery that evolved us and all living things. The expanded consciousness that results from serial top-talent *flow* states cascades into upgrades to conceptual, abstract, deductive, strategic, and big-picture thinking, environmental scanning and pattern recognition, and the ability to capitalize on the interconnectedness of all things.

THE BIOLOGICALLY MAXIMIZED JOB SEARCH

Executive Job Search before biologically maximized: the need for proactive serial job replacement in all career strategy.

The methods, challenges, and damages of today's job search protocol are examined so that a biologically maximized replacement strategy presented in the next article may be appreciated. The inefficiencies of today's job search protocol may leave the majority of executive job searchers jobless for 1 to 2 years. If we can dramatically shorten that time and remove the challenges, risks, dangers, and damages of the current process, then a new career strategy will become possible.

If we had a high-speed, high-growth, high-impact job search protocol, an accelerated career strategy of proactive serial job replacement would be viable. Serial job replacement offers tremendous opportunities for growth, wealth creation, and impact across your career. This new process for accelerating job search is the same methodology for profound performance for achieving any goal in partnership with the maximizing machinery.

Proactive Serial Job Replacement – A Career Game-Changer

This article introduces the promised revolutionary job search protocol that is exhilarating, accelerated, nourishing, growth-inciting, targeted, and acutely accurate in its selection of your ideal job. It has the speed and efficiency to enable the breakthrough career strategy of the century: Proactive Serial Job Replacement. Now job breaks may be proactively sought for accelerated advancement, wealth creation, and growth with the knowledge that job replacement when you are ready will not be a problem.

THE BIOLOGICALLY MAXIMIZED CORPORATION

The New Corporate Maximums: Biology – the competitive advantage no one foresaw

Biological mechanisms maximize human systems. Corporations maximize human systems. When the two join forces, every best practice for corporate success is revolutionized. Few companies have foreseen the magnitude of this pending transformation to management science. The corporate landscape will be littered with those who fail to make the leap before their competition.

3

THE SECRET CAREER STRATEGY OF THE WORLD'S MOST SUCCESSFUL EXECUTIVES

Many of us have followed an externally driven career strategy. Once we take our first career job, we choose the next to capitalize on the first. With repetition, we soon inadvertently commit to a career ladder for our increasing rewards. We compromise to conform to the requirements of each ladder rung to ensure our climb.

In contrast, those most successful in achieving the rewards to which so many aspire appear to be internally driven. Examine the lives of super-achievers Bill Gates (Microsoft co-founder), Steve Jobs and Steve Wozniak (Apple co-founders), Mark Zuckerberg (Facebook founder), Larry Page and Sergey Brin (Google co-founders), and Jeff Bezos (Amazon founder) for this common thread. Rather than compromising to fit into the next job up the ladder, they create or take the job that provides the ideal next growth-and-achievement context.

This first article in the series will introduce you to how a biologically maximized career strategy will

- pull you ahead with addictive drives for growth and achievement,
- cause new functionality to emerge, and
- have you operating at peak performance and *beyond*.

The Pull of Paid Play

For our seven super-achievers, the addictive play of their childhood continued as the paid play of adulthood. The movie, *The Social Network*, gives us a glimpse into the addictive play that engaged Zuckerberg's greatest talents in the creation of Facebook. Bill Gates' addictive software wizardry was irresistible play that got him into trouble as a child until it got him into Microsoft and money.

While Bezos' programming expertise might have launched Amazon, it is his captivation with incessant invention – his true paid play – that has sustained Amazon's global prominence. His brilliance for creative solutions and his need for their challenge were evident from a pre-school age. Programming, computers and the digital world became tools for his invention.

This resulted in Bezos' change of venue for his drives to invention from physics to computer science and electrical engineering at Princeton as he narrowed to compliance with his biological bias. This foreshadowed a further refinement of venue for his addictive invention drives in leaving the safety of the corporate world for the unprecedented world of pure invention that became Amazon.

To others, this addictive play would be work. But to our super-achievers, this is irresistible play they enjoy so much that they would do it for free. It is work that is intrinsically rewarding. For all of them and for all of us, *it is the specific "work" that each of us would want to do if we had unlimited resources and freedom.* It is the work or play that we are innately predisposed to do. It is thus the grist of our greatest legacy and contribution to the world.

Imagine a career propelled not by discipline or external enforcers but by internal biological drives to use and improve our most addictive and rewarding strengths.

Built into the drives to this addictive play is the pressure to stretch to apply one's best talents to creations at increasingly more challenging and impactful levels. We have evolved addictive drives that biologically bias us to use and improve our greatest strengths. *We are biologically biased to peak performance.* It is advantageous to the survival of the species. The more you comply with the addictive drives we have evolved for it, the more you want to comply with them.

The addictive drives entice one along a lifetime continuum of growth-and-creation iterations: growing oneself to grow one's creative impact on the world. Aligning one's career strategy with this biological bias yields superior performance and a commensurate increase in internal and external rewards. *It is the ultimate formula for the maximized career and the maximized life.*

Jeff Bezos was surrounded by gifted physicists at Princeton. While his marks were good, he knew he did not love the work as they did. He was not maximized by operating in his field of addictive paid play as they were. They offered him the model of a maximized career and life founded on their greatest strengths. Jeff shifted his academic major and his career to achieve this model. His seemingly multi-faceted career has been one of continuous narrowing to the addictive "invention" drives at his biological foundation. This is the maximized career strategy promoted in this blog series.

Magic happens when you stretch your best talents to more impactful achievements over long periods of time. You repeatedly experience an altered state of consciousness that psychologist Csikszentmihalyi calls *flow*. Attention is 100% focused on the activity at hand. Peak performance and growth are built in. Time, space, and even self-awareness cease to exist. *Flow* is intrinsically rewarding. It too is an addictive drive that will raise your baseline functionality as it did with our super-seven.

The Triggering of Cascading Functionality Upgrades

Repetitive experience of *flow* arising specifically from the application of your key talents to meaningful work will launch an accelerated growth continuum. New functionality and meta-skills will emerge. Therefore, the addictive play of our seven super-achievers inadvertently had them operating at peak performance while triggering continuous increases to their baseline functionality.

For example, the *flow* state associated with using and improving your key talents expands one's perspective. As consciousness expands, the interconnections of all human systems become visible. The potential for a unified humanity becomes apparent. Each of the visions of our seven super-achievers was informed by their view of the world from their bouts of expanded consciousness in *flow*.

This shared perspective pulled Amazon, Microsoft, Apple, Facebook, and Google through the interim steps we have seen to date to unify and advance our world. Ponder the breadth of thinking of Page and Brin based on their Google mission statement: *"to organize the world's information and make it universally accessible and useful."* A mission "to set up a search engine" could never have inspired the diversification and impact that Google has achieved.

Expanded consciousness causes a chain reaction. Cognitive capabilities increase. Upgrades occur in conceptual skills, systems thinking, relational thinking, big-picture thinking, pattern recognition, the use of models, theories, and inferences, and abilities for creative and opportunistic problem-solving, adaptivity, and inventiveness. Does this remind you of the capabilities that emerged over time in our super-seven?

Performance beyond your Potential

The addictive drives that promote the application of one's strengths have evolved as survival drives for the individual and the species. They are part of a network of internal and external forces that have evolved throughout nature to maximize living systems for survival. They are an extension of the same forces that keep our internal organs and systems operating at their maximum.

Most of our seven never separated from nature's network of maximizing forces. Others, such as Jeff Bezos, re-merged when they turned themselves over to their natural growth-and-creation continuum. When we comply with our talent-promoting addictive drives we re-integrate with nature's drives for maximizing systems. *We shift into overdrive.*

Circuits inside of us are *completed* by circuits outside of us to increase our performance for survival. Our capabilities are extended by nature's capabilities. We can perform beyond our potential. As intelligent as our super-seven are, it is their slips into this internal-external *overdrive* that resulted in their moments of brilliance. Even those of average intelligence can achieve the genius of savant status in this biologically compliant state.

An upgraded modus operandi for the Everyman

The new method of operation examined in this blog series is a paradigm shift. It is the true secret career strategy of the world's most successful executives. It explains their success in an unprecedented way that everyone may replicate. It provides one with access to levels of success one may not have thought possible for oneself. It offers a new route for each of us to make our most meaningful contribution to the advance of the world.

But it also hints at a future modus operandi for humanity. These seven men did not just discover a better career strategy. They did not just advance humanity on a better path. They modeled a new level of peak performance accessible to every human being. Explore your biologically maximized career potential in future blogs to push the envelope on your own lifetime achievements and rewards.

Steve Jobs in his 2005 Stanford University graduation speech: *"I'm convinced that the only thing that kept me going was that I loved what I did. You've got to find what you love. If you haven't found it yet, keep looking. Don't settle. As with all matters of the heart, you'll know when you find it. And, like any great relationship, it just gets better and better as the years roll on. So keep looking until you find it. Don't settle."*

4

THE NEW CAREER MAXIMUMS – Part One

Have you settled for too little?

PART ONE: RELEASE INTERNAL POTENTIAL
Internal aspects of your biologically maximized career – new
meta-skills; sudden knowledge, genius, breakthroughs, and
creativity; whole-brain savantism; top-talent *flow* and growth;
and aligning career and growth paths for paid growth and paid
play.

PART TWO: BORROW EXTERNAL POTENTIAL
External support for your biologically maximized career –
Borrow from nature and surrounding systems: predictability,
power, resources, information, functionality, creativity, growth,
and frontiering™.
Your biologically maximized career – serial breakthrough
synthesis; serial top-talent *flow*; serial frontiering™; trend
integration and mass synchronization; synergies and multi-
system achieving.

Executives are charged with maximizing corporate resources for corporate gain. Many mechanisms, processes, procedures and systems have been put in place to discover and achieve maximum returns on corporate resources. However, one's personal asset maximization is seldom the focus of career or life strategies.

Few identify their maximum possible career and then pursue it. Few pursue their maximum lifetime contribution to the advance of the world nor the commensurate tangible and intangible rewards. However, this is a common regret on the career front for the majority from their retirement rocking chair.

WHAT IS YOUR CAREER MAXIMUM?

Before I introduce some new potential career maximums, take a moment to determine what you currently consider your highest possible life's work. The questions below may spur your thinking:

1. If you had total freedom and unlimited resources, what creations or footprints would you want to leave over your lifetime?
2. What work would you dedicate yourself to do to contribute to or advance our world?
3. Generically, what might your maximum career look like based solely on the continuous application and improvement of your strongest, most rewarding talents?
4. To what meaningful work would you dedicate your life in the absence of all impediments and distractions?
5. If we removed all of the demands of family, finances, and the challenges life throws at you, what would be your ultimate career?
6. If we stripped away all competing "careers" such as parenting, supporting one's family, a hobby, or a cause, what would be your maximum creative expression? What are the creations for which you would like to receive your income?
7. What are your maximum possible lifetime achievements?
8. What could be your maximum possible career legacy?

In an unrestricted vision of lifetime career maximization, each of us would want to do meaningful work we are passionate about. We would want to grow in our ability to do that work. We would want to continuously increase its value and impact. We would want to apply our greatest talents – the talents we most enjoy – at their maximum to the work which would be most valued by the world and by ourselves. This is the work which will bring the most tangible and intangible rewards.

In the previous chapter, we learned about a biologically addictive '*paid play*' that pulled seven executives to success: Bill Gates (Microsoft co-founder), Steve Jobs and Steve Wozniak (Apple co-founders), Mark Zuckerberg (Facebook founder), Larry Page and Sergey Brin (Google co-founders), and Jeff Bezos (Amazon founder).

Because this '*paid play*' is driven by addictive drives, the more you do this kind of work, the more you want to do it. And the more you do it, the better you get at it. Eventually you will achieve breakthroughs that advance your paid-play domain. The drives which biologically predispose us to our field of '*paid play*' *pulled* our seven iconic founders to superior performance and accelerated growth. The result was performance, throughput, and breakthroughs that far exceeded what they could have achieved through the controlling *push* of discipline. These superstars were internally or biologically driven.

Let's have a look at some other biological maximums that you may not have thought to include in your previous determination of your career maximum. Let's look at some of the new carecr maximums that will dramatically upgrade today's state-of-the-art career strategy.

What is your biological career potential?

Strip away for the moment all of your competing life goals and struggles. What do you have the potential to accomplish if you applied full power to a singular focus? What is your true career potential? What does nature consider your maximum?

A career based on our biological maximum would be dedicated to work to which we are "biologically predisposed to excel" and "biologically predisposed to crave." Such maximum work would require us to apply our strongest, most rewarding talents to their maximum. Our expertise with those talents would continuously upgrade at our maximum possible growth rate.

Our peak performance would be committed to our most valued work. This is the work for which we will receive the greatest intrinsic and extrinsic rewards. A biologically maximized career would be defined by the pull of our most addictive "paid play" and "paid growth." It would be propelled by drives not discipline.

However, more than this, a career based on our biological maximums would comply with and capitalize on the maximizing mechanisms and processes that have evolved human beings. It would have us reintegrate with the flow of systems synergistically maximizing each other. It would not have us dissipating energy to oppose that flow. It would exploit maximizing forces and co-evolving systems so that their capabilities could be added to ours to enable us to achieve beyond our internal potential.

This is precisely what we observe in the careers of the seven accomplished founders of Google, Amazon, Apple, Microsoft, and Facebook.

Exploit biological maximizing for a career beyond your innate potential

The human biological imperative seeks the maximization of the individual and the species for survival. Nature routinely, perpetually, and impartially maximizes human systems for survival. Over generations, a *"machinery"* has evolved inside and outside of us to promote this maximization.

Inside, we may observe it maximizing systems within our body for health and performance. Think especially of the adaptivity of our immune and nervous systems to external elements, for example. Outside, we see this machinery maximizing stock markets, and economic and sociological systems.

It is only logical to assume that the same forces maximizing systems within a biological ecosystem would also act on each of us. We are a part of the larger maximizing machinery that evolved us. If we knew how to capitalize on this machinery, we could raise the bar on our career potential. We could extend our capabilities with these maximizing mechanisms, systems, processes, and intelligence to operate beyond what we might perceive is our inborn potential.

Only by reintegrating with this maximizing process will we know our true potential and hence our career potential.

1. What could you accomplish if you spent decades operating beyond your potential in your strongest domain?

2. What would be your career maximum if you spent a lifetime conscripting other systems to achieve bigger goals than you are capable of attaining on your own?

3. Where would your career take you if you rejoined the massive orchestration of all biological systems?

4. If you learned how to exploit this maximizing machinery for your own system and your career, could you not also apply it to maximize any human system to achieve beyond its potential?

5. Could you not extrapolate the same process to your subordinates, your company, your family, your child, a market, a country, or the system of humanity as a whole?

6. How much more profoundly capable would you be as an executive leading multi-system companies in multi-system markets? This too will increase your career maximum.

7. What business can succeed against a competitor harnessing the maximizing mechanisms of evolution?
8. What leader would choose to operate contrary to the direction of the evolutionary flow?

Let's look first at some aspects of maximizing internally in *Part One*. In Part Two, we will look at some of the new career maximums possible by exploiting the external portion of the maximizing machinery.

Flashes of genius and sudden savantism

Our seven super-achievers experienced frequent flashes of genius beyond their potential as they complied with their biologically maximized careers. With some tweaks of biology, it is possible for even those of normal intelligence or less to experience those same spikes of genius.

Let's compare these moments of brilliance to savant syndrome for a moment. Savants exhibit extreme talent in the wake of profound disabilities. A person with below normal intelligence is able to display an exceptional if not prodigious talent or ability in a specific area. Savants operate at levels that would be unusual even for normal people.

Many were introduced to this exceptional intellectual capacity by the savant star, Raymond, in the popular movie, *Rain Man* (1988). The inspiration for Dustin Hoffman's role came from Kim Peek or "Kimputer" who was born without the thick band of axons connecting the left and right hemispheres. Kim is capable of incredible feats of memory and calculation. He can recall over 7,600 books and has a nearly complete and up-to-date knowledge of world history, area codes, zip codes, roads and highways and much more.

Savantism appears to emerge when birth, injury, or dementia removes left-brain control of the right brain. There is evidence that the brain "re-wires" itself to not only avoid damaged areas but to compensate for them. The exceptional abilities observed in those who acquire savantism later in life do not emerge because of a sudden *creation* of skills. Rather, experts believe that what occurs is a *release of skills and talents already present.*

Since savant syndrome can be acquired, scientists believe that all of us, theoretically, have the potential to become savants. It appears that each of us may have a *super-talent territory* or *savant domain* in which flashes of genius beyond our normal intelligence can be achieved. Savantism suggests a greater potential of the human brain and how talent and genius may manifest. Since flashes of genius would upgrade anyone's career maximum, let's examine some alternative means to release our own savantism with some adjustments to our modus operandi.

5

THE NEW CAREER MAXIMUMS
– Part One – continued

Have you settled for too little?

PART ONE: RELEASE INTERNAL POTENTIAL
Internal aspects of your biologically maximized career – new meta-skills; sudden knowledge, genius, breakthroughs, and creativity; whole-brain savantism; top-talent *flow* and growth; and aligning career and growth paths for paid growth and paid play.

Whole-Brain Savantism

Most of the known savants have been left-brain weak. This suggests that the level of left-brain intelligence will not determine who will experience the flashes of genius we observe in the lives of our seven super-achievers.

The left hemisphere of the brain provides logic, reasoning, analysis and objectivity. It is verbal and rational. Our right hemisphere is the hub for creativity, novelty, intuition, subjectivity, pattern recognition, and holistic and divergent thinking. It is your nonverbal and intuitive brain. It thinks in patterns. It comprehends pictures and "whole things." It controls visual, spatial and relational thinking. It does not comprehend reductions, numbers, letters, or words.

Our goal is not the elimination of the left brain as in savants. However, the current scientific evidence suggests we will still need the left brain to release control of the right brain. This can be more advantageously accomplished by an increase in the right brain so that a partnership of both hemispheres can give us whole-brain operation. Our goal is a synergy in which the whole brain is greater than the sum of its two parts.

One might try allowing the left and right brain to operate simultaneously in parallel or synchronously to achieve this equal partnership. However, the right brain may be better freed for aspiring novice whole-brainers if one consciously uses alternating applications of right brain then left brain to any project. This will free the creative right brain for insights and genius without sacrificing left-brain logic and functionality.

Writers, for example, could do one or more freehand, unedited, and unrestricted right-brain passes for creativity, insights, and genius to develop concepts or story. A left-brain pass would address the logic, editing, grammar and spelling. Executives could do the same for developing strategic or tactical plans. However, whole-brain operation is easier to achieve than one might think. Other options are built into us as part of the maximizing machinery.

Whole-brain operation is a biological maximum. It is therefore better for the survival of the individual and the species. Consequently, we have evolved a biological bias to it. Many mechanisms, processes, and urges have evolved to promote whole-brain operation. *Flow* state is one important example internally that will be discussed below. External mechanisms that promote whole-brain flashes of genius will be revealed in Part Two. We can learn to bypass or overcome the cultural and corporate interferences that pressure left-brain control.

The *"Eureka!"* or *"Aha!"* effect

When normal intelligence is applied to action, implement, or operationalize your periodic "smart events" or breakthroughs, the sum total of your career performance will increase. Sometimes it only takes one breakthrough to make a career and change the world. Our seven iconic founders experienced *serial breakthroughs as a way of life*. You can too. Let's examine internally and externally (Part Two) what will make that new career maximum possible.

The *"Eureka!" or "Aha!" effect* refers to the common human experience of suddenly understanding a previously incomprehensible problem or concept. If you source only partial solutions to a problem, then you are likely in the midst of a left-brain reasoning process rather than a right-brain *"Aha!"* event. This is about sudden knowledge, sudden knowing, and sudden access to new information.

"Insight" is the official psychological term in problem solving for instances in which a previously unsolvable puzzle becomes suddenly clear and obvious. Neuroscience and brain scans have located the part of the right brain in which true insights occur. The anterior superior temporal gyrus of the right hemisphere is where remote and unconnected associations are brought together and linked. As you will learn, the gyrus along with the rest of the right brain is activated by *flow* states.

It is interesting that anecdotal evidence records rapid experience of *"Eureka!"* events or seeming all-knowingness during near-death experiences (NDE) when cultural interferences have been minimized. The brain seemingly clicks into its maximized state of coherence and synergy especially with respect to the *super-talent* or *savant domain* associated with the strongest talents of each individual. NDErs experience savantism. For some, the savantism and bias for this domain survives the near-death experience.

There is an addictiveness to the highs of *"Aha!"* experiences that pulls you to pursue them again and again. As they increase in number, the baseline of your intelligence and functionality increases. Also, your knowledge of your *savant domain* goes up with each breakthrough. Your career maximum augments accordingly. In no time at all you are penetrating new frontiers in your field just as the seven super-achievers did with Google, Amazon, Facebook, Microsoft, and Apple. Have you been settling?

Flow maximizes instantly

As mentioned, one of the internal mechanisms in the maximizing machinery is *flow* state. Psychologist, Mihalyi Csikszentmihalyi, describes *flow* as our optimal and our most enjoyable experience in his book of the same name (1991). *Flow* is our maximized state. All the body's resources are trained on the current intrinsically rewarding work. The biological imperative, then, will seek to have us operate in *flow* 100% of the time. Because *flow* is an addictive, peak-performing and peak-growth state, it is one of the key drivers of human evolution.

To experience this wonderfully rewarding state of *flow*, one must be stretched beyond one's previous capabilities. Therefore, a maximum- or *flow*-seeking career will go beyond peak performance to peak growth. We are not only biologically biased to peak performance but to increasing the baseline functionality of that peak performance. How smart of the human species to have evolved an addictive maximum state that draws us to perpetually transcend ourselves. Accordingly, the maximum of a *flow*-focused career would continuously rise as well.

Your maximum *flow*: top-talent flow

All *flow* states are not equal in achieving savantism or your biological and career maximums. Maximization promotes peak performance from peak strengths for peak expression, peak impact, and peak rewards. Your true maximum *flow* state will therefore emerge from using and improving your strongest, most addicting, and most rewarding talents in the domain most facilitating for and valuing of their use. I call these extended periods of operating at your talent-based maximum "top-talent *flows*."

If you were going to release your inner savant or super-talents, this is the territory in which it/they would emerge. Just as in savantism, the skills of extraordinary performance are already biologically present rather than having to be cultivated. Most who acquired savantism later in life never demonstrated their savant domain or super-talent territory prior to the injury or dementia which damaged the left brain thus releasing their right brain to savantism.

Since top-talent *flow* is our true maximum, we are biologically biased to pursue this intrinsically gratifying state. This is the *flow* state most supported by mechanisms, processes, and drives enmeshed within the internal-external maximizing machinery. It is dramatically more powerful and transformative than any other form of *flow*. Accelerated growth, breakthrough creations, new meta-skills, and flashes of genius and savantism are significantly more prevalent.

Exponential magic happens in your top-talent *flows*. Now imagine how powerful and transformed our seven founders would be after spending years in these transformative *flow* states which emerge while they are applying their greatest strengths. This is what I believe caused the significant accomplishments of our seven achievers. In many cases, these *flow* states enabled achievements beyond their innate intelligence.

A majority of the seven had computer, internet, and software work in their childhood or early careers. Computer programming is particularly compelling for inciting top-talent *flow* states. Colloquially, they are called "hack mode," a Zen-like state of total focus. They are so captivating that many programmers blissfully program all night and forget to eat. They are so addictive that they not only became the "paid play" of many of our seven founders but fostered an industry of computer and video games. This is how I believe these seven were *pulled* to their achievements rather than *pressured* by a superior discipline or outside force to achieve them. This suggests an alternative career strategy for those highly disciplined executives who have achieved neither the intrinsic nor extrinsic rewards that they seek.

Sudden savantism through top-talent *flow*

A person in *flow* state has alpha brainwaves not unlike those of a Zen monk in meditation. When in this alpha-intensive state, we can retain cognitive consciousness for far longer than the few seconds of duration characteristic of normal, beta-wave consciousness. This extended consciousness equips us to solve complex problems, follow extended chains of reasoning, and take on tasks that we simply cannot fit into the transient episodes of normal beta-wave arousal.

Flow states also seem to be more conducive than normal consciousness to activation of the right anterior superior temporal gyrus, the region of the brain associated with intuitive leaps and sudden insight. It appears that the chatter of beta-wave activity in normal consciousness somehow competes with our *"Aha!"* circuitry. In addition, the requirement for stretching beyond one's previous capabilities to enter into *flow*, upgrades capabilities and performance towards savant stature.

However, the real power of top-talent *flow* is that it releases our whole-brain genius to full power. The right brain is freed from left-brain domination in this maximal *flow* state. Thus, the triggers of acquired savant syndrome are duplicated. Whole-brain *flow* incites the perfect left-brain and right-brain synergy.

Growth through top-talent *flow*

Flow is a peak-performance and peak-growth state. Growth is built into *flow* and particularly top-talent *flow* because a) *flow* is so fulfilling that it becomes addictive, b) achieving this intrinsically rewarding *flow* state requires us to be stretched beyond our previous capabilities, and c) *flow* is a transforming state. Learning adds new information to one's existing system. However, top-talent *flow* actually reformulates or re-wires one's system with new functionality and new potential.

This is what I believe our seven super-achievers experienced. As a result, they spent their careers operating at peak growth. Year after year they raised their baseline functionality and the level of impact of their creations and achievements faster than most of us would. This is what happened with Google, Amazon, Microsoft, Facebook and Apple. Not all of the founders are as brilliant as what they created. However, by adhering to the domain to which they are biologically predisposed, achievement beyond expectation was possible.

Year after year, their meta-skills and "*Aha!*" events increased in top-talent *flow,* so they not only operated beyond their potential, they raised that potential. Consciousness expanded. Conceptual skills increased. So even if Gates, Jobs, Wozniak, Bezos, Brin, Page, and Zuckerberg did not start with genius, it would likely emerge over time. The skills and meta-skills that developed in the savant domain would spill over into other facets of their life to raise overall performance and intelligence.

For example, one's ability to break through frontier after frontier in one's savant domain would provide expertise for penetrating new or unknown territory in other disciplines in which one's performance was innately inferior. What would your career maximum be if you never diluted your savant strengths and never left your savant domain? This is what our seven iconic founders share and demonstrate for us.

New meta-skills from extensive top-talent *flow* experience

Elevations in consciousness will increase our functionality and meta-skills. Cognitive skills, for example, will advance. Operational intelligence will be improved by upgrades in abstract thinking, conceptual thinking, big-picture thinking, systems thinking, strategic thinking, mental agility, adaptivity, pattern recognition, trend perception, environmental scanning, problem re-framing, and ambiguity resolution. Notice the addition of many right-brain capabilities in particular.

Few educational programs have been effective in developing any of these meta-skills. However, they upgrade collectively as a paradigm shift when we reintegrate into the maximizing machinery and experience serial top-talent *flows*. These kinds of meta-skills are pivotal to executive performance. Executive career maximums therefore will upgrade significantly with this proposed maximum modus operandi.

Paid growth, paid play – Make your natural growth path your career path

The biologically maximum career would consist of a series of top-talent *flow* experiences in which you would continuously a) surpass your previous performance and b) re-wire your system to raise not only your baseline functionality but also your potential.

Our growth path, then, will be a nonlinear amplification or expansion or intensification of our strongest talents to increase their power to impact reality and the precision with which they create. It will be a growth path in which we are constantly breaking through new frontiers of knowledge, skill, and reality

OUR NATURAL GROWTH PATH AS
OUR MAXIMUM CAREER PATH
Excerpted from the video program:
Leadering – Paradigm Shift to
Peak Legacy (Lauren Holmes 2011)
Figure 1

impact in our savant domain. This accelerated growth path would thus define our maximum career path, biologically speaking.

We have a biological predisposition towards enjoying the application of certain talents more than others. Therefore, your maximum is innate. Hence, your growth path will be innate given that nature only seeks to maximize systems for survival. Therefore, your ideal career strategy is one of being paid to grow your most fun talents and to apply them to larger and more meaningful projects (see figure 1).

Read *Part Two* to learn more about external maximizing mechanisms and their synergy with internal one's such as those discussed here in *Part One*.

6

THE NEW CAREER MAXIMUMS – Part Two

Have you settled for too little?

PART TWO: BORROW EXTERNAL POTENTIAL
External support for your biologically maximized career –
Borrow from nature and surrounding systems:
predictability, power, resources, information, functionality,
creativity, growth, and frontiering™.
Your biologically maximized career – serial breakthrough
synthesis; serial top-talent *flow*; serial frontiering™; trend
integration and mass synchronization; synergies and multi-
system achieving.

Our examination of the biologically maximized career continues. In *Part One*, we examined the new career maximums possible from exploiting internal elements of the maximizing process that has evolved the human species. In *Part Two*, we will discover how the external portion of this process may be exploited to achieve new career maximums. The external maximizing process provides the fuel for the internal processes. That fuel is *information*. It also provides direction, power, borrowable capabilities and functionality, predictability, synergies, and synchronization with world trends.

We have been examining the careers of seven icons for commonalities: Bill Gates (Microsoft), Steve Jobs and Steve Wozniak (Apple), Mark Zuckerberg (Facebook), Larry Page and Sergey Brin (Google), and Jeff Bezos (Amazon). What they share is a biologically maximized career. Discover these new career maximums for yourself. Their level of world-changing legacy may then become yours.

BREAKTHROUGH SYNTHESIS

There is a singular dynamic transaction within nature's maximizing process which ensures not just the survival of living systems but their synchronized and synergistic advance. This dynamic is the underlying energetic for growth, adaptation, creativity, and even evolution. It is an information creation dynamic I will call *breakthrough synthesis* since something novel is always created. **Breakthrough synthesis re-combines existing information systems to create a new information system.**

Brilliant breakthroughs

The newly manufactured information systems emerge from this breakthrough synthesis as "sudden nonlinear creations" or "*quantum leaps.*" The highly desirable quantum leaps from *Part One* all rely on *breakthrough synthesis*: flashes of genius, "Aha!" and "Eureka!" events, sudden insight, sudden knowledge, sudden *savantism*, sudden creativity, creative inspirations, intuitive leaps, epiphanies, and enlightenment.

These desirable breakthroughs all require the right information fuel at the right time. This fuel is provided by the external portion of the maximizing machinery. Even a few such breakthroughs may be sufficient to create a life-changing or even world-changing career. However, a career of serial breakthroughs may lead to cumulative legacies substantially beyond one's perceived potential. Even those of only ordinary intelligence and with little ability to innovate likely have sufficient smarts to re-combine information pieces placed right in front of them by the maximizing process to generate flashes of genius.

Biological breakthrough synthesis

Breakthrough synthesis is not a new tool invented for career advance. It is a key biological dynamic of maximizing, adaptation, growth, creativity, and evolution. It synthesizes the creative solutions to the everyday challenges to maximizing living systems for survival. It is nature's preferred form of creativity. Consequently, it is available all around us for us to conscript to achieve bigger goals better. We can extend our creativity with nature's to achieve beyond our potential.

Breakthrough synthesis is evident in the genetic synthesis which re-combines the information of our parents and the generations before to create each of us? Breakthrough synthesis generates the proteins that are the foundation of all living systems. The synthesis of amino acids into proteins and nucleic acids into genetic material are fundamental to life. The promising future from these two examples is that they too once appeared to scientists as sudden leaps to a whole which is greater than the sum of its parts. One day we may know enough about what created our "Eureka!" events that we can make them routine for everyone.

It would be illogical to assume that we, as individual human beings, are exempt from this breakthrough synthesis theme that is advancing all living systems. Reintegrating into the maximizing machinery that evolved us will restore breakthrough synthesis to us as a career tool for exceptional performance. But more than this, we, too, are information systems which may be re-combined to create new information systems. We may therefore play a role as the information fuel, the catalyst, or the creation once we allow ourselves to be orchestrated by the maximizing machinery helping all living systems to survive.

Flow is our internal breakthrough synthesis

This same breakthrough synthesis drives our shifts into our peak-performance, peak-growth *flow* states. It is not by accident that the activity of the anterior superior temporal gyrus in the right brain increases during *flow*. This is where remote and unconnected associations are brought together and linked in breakthrough synthesis. In *Part One* we learned about new career maximums such as this one that are possible through the internal portion of the maximizing machinery. The external portion provides the fuel for this internal breakthrough synthesis: the information.

An increase in career-changing breakthroughs is built into *flow* state. This is especially true of our top-talent *flow* states that arise from the application of our strongest, most preferred talents to our most meaningful challenges. A shift into *flow* is a leap to maximization. *Flow* states therefore automatically integrate us into the maximizing machinery. The external portion of the machinery then orchestrates us to the right place and time for the information to fuel our internal breakthrough synthesis. Examine your past top-talent *flows* to view this process in action. You now have a formula for generating breakthroughs at will with which to excel.

Growth internally / Creativity externally

Sudden insights and *flow* states are not alone in being driven by breakthrough synthesis.
- *Growth* is breakthrough synthesis applied internally.
- *Creativity* is breakthrough synthesis applied externally.

Inward-facing growth is the combining of new information with your existing internal information to create a new you. Your personal information structure is replaced with a more advanced one. In exactly the same way, outward-facing creativity incorporates new information into the information structure of the world system to generate a new world system. Creativity is "world growth," so to speak, no matter who is creating something new.

Exploit *maximization-linked* coincidences

Coincidences are yet another of the sudden leaps to new knowledge discussed in the previous section. They too are products of breakthrough synthesis. A single coincidence has been responsible for some of the most spectacular careers. However, a coincidence is also the information fuel for breakthrough synthesis. Three to seven coincidences or information systems are usually sufficient for the re-mix to create a significant new information system: an *"Aha!"* or *"Eureka!"* event, for example.

Coincidences are both the fuel and the product of breakthrough synthesis. Fortunately, integrating into the maximizing machinery will exponentially explode your experience of coincidences. How delightful! These coincidences, of course, will fuel a plethora of career-making breakthrough syntheses. Your career maximum will increase commensurately. How one cultivates these catalytic coincidences is an article in itself. However, here is a brief introduction.

Officially, a *coincidence* is the simultaneous occurrence of events that appear significantly related but have no discernible causal connection. However, the *coincidences* that you will be experiencing with this proposed new career maximizing methodology *will* be causally linked to the maximizing process for your system. These are *maximization-linked* coincidences. Because they will seem serendipitous, the term 'coincidence' still works for our purposes.

However, they are actually *co-maximizations* or synergies among fellow maximizers. Living systems grab information from each other to fuel breakthrough synthesis to generate creative solutions to maximizing or adaptation challenges. The new information systems created by the re-mix appear as the coincidences in your life. However, these created coincidences are also the fuel for the next round of breakthrough syntheses or maximizing. In effect, breakthrough synthesis *is* the maximizing process. It both creates coincidences or information systems and uses them.

Accordingly, a cluster of coincidences will always indicate the flow of the maximizing process in your reality. The closer you are to your maximized state, the more compliant you will be to being orchestrated by the maximizing machinery to the right information at the right time for breakthroughs. The self-ordering nature of the machinery will then group you with the systems best able to provide you with the information you need next. This will increase the volume and quality of the information coincidences that you will experience. Your breakthroughs will increase commensurately.

You may recall from *Part One* that your maximized state is top-talent *flow* or a *flow* state that derives from applying your strongest, most preferred, talents to the field or application that is most meaningful to you. If the coincidences in your life are sparse or nonexistent, then you likely have moved out of the flow of the maximizing process. You are not maximized. You are sitting idly on the riverbank with the other unmaximized living systems. You will have no information fuel for the quantum leaps to career-making breakthroughs, insights, and flashes of genius.

These coincidences are not psychological or RAS events

These *maximization-linked* coincidences are not simply psychologically meaningful events as psychologist Carl Jung proposed in his 1920s' definition of "synchronicities." These are not simply psychological transactions whereby you confer shared meaning on unrelated events. These are true physical events which result from the shared information pieces from your co-maximizing partners. These "coincidences" are physical symptoms of the underlying dynamic order of a singular process which might be called "*maximizing*" or "*adaptation*" or "*growth*" or "*creativity*" or "*creation*" or "*emergence*" or "*self-ordering*" or "*problem-solving*" or "*breakthrough synthesis.*"

Nor are these *coincidences* or *information quantum leaps* or *co-maximizations* the result of your *reticular activating system (RAS)* seeing whatever you have been focused on. Your RAS is your information filter or gatekeeper. It is the reason why, when you buy the car you have been researching, you will see that model everywhere. It has evolved to filter thousands of items per second to select the information that you need for survival. Your RAS may help you to identify the best coincidences for your next breakthrough synthesis. However, it obviously does not create those coincidences. It is filtering true physical events.

7

THE NEW CAREER MAXIMUMS
– Part Two – Continued

PART TWO: BORROW EXTERNAL POTENTIAL
External support for your biologically maximized career –
Borrow from nature and surrounding systems: predictability,
power, resources, information, functionality, creativity, growth,
and frontiering™.

THE SCIENCE BEHIND BREAKTHROUGH SYNTHESIS

P*art One* and *Part Two* contain biological discoveries and theories by the author resulting from extensive executive interviews, examinations, and experimentations which applied scientific method to the lives of individual executives and, especially, multinational executives. This has resulted in a new biologically maximized modus operandi for human beings which bypasses cultural interference.

This new way of operating prescribes full integration into biological mechanisms and processes inside and outside of us which have evolved to work together synergistically but which have been culturally overruled. I have created a link to material that hints at some relevant science to explain in laymen's terms what enables the breakthrough synthesis to work. Hopefully, this brief description will suffice until separate articles may be written with more details about the relevant scientific discoveries. (See Chapter 5).

MASS SYNCHRONIZATION: Trend creation and exploitation
Mass maximization generates mass synchronization. Mass maximization provides the ideal synchronized direction for the

majority of living systems to survive. Here are some of the ways this synchronization is created and may be exploited to increase your career potential:

1. The dance of systems maximizing and re-maximizing to each other and their shared context serves to orchestrate a synchronized advance of living systems. It orchestrates synergies which further synchronize systems. Mass synchronization groups potentially synergistic systems together to better share resources, assets and functionality. Your career potential is extended and supplemented by these other systems.

2. These synergies include information sharing for the breakthrough synthesis that will solve respective maximization challenges. Complying with the maximizing flow will orchestrate you to the right place at the right time to source the information you need to fuel your career-making breakthroughs.

3. Clusters of coincidences will always identify the direction of the synchronized flow. You will always know where the flow of the maximizing machinery is in your context or your company's context by the clustering of coincidences and facilitating events.

4. In a world of systems nested within systems, order nested within order, and emergence nested within emergence, the orchestration of compliant systems into synchronization defines world trends. Complying with the maximizing process then will keep careers, companies, and, indeed, any human systems, at the leading edge of world trends.

5. An added benefit, of course, is that being compliant or being part of the synchronization will ensure that you will also not be fighting against trends as you try to get ahead. You will not be impeded from achieving your career maximums. Careers therefore benefit from being integrated into current

trends. Careers gain by complying with the flow to maximization of the larger system of which we are all a part.

6. If you find yourself constantly hitting blocks to your progress or negative frustrating events, you have either fallen out of the mass synchronization or not found it yet. When you tap into the ongoing maximizing quantum leap process all around you, you can be catapulted to your work or career goals. It will become apparent how your career may be dramatically amplified and accelerated.

7. Mass synchronization allows you to extend your capabilities with those of other systems and the maximizing machinery itself. You will then be able to operate beyond your potential to achieve new career maximums.

Merging into nature's maximizing process causes synchronization as a byproduct. Synchronization will keep your career and your company leading edge. It is also a potential new leadership tool for keeping any human systems – companies, countries, and humanity – moving in lock-step towards your goals. It is one of several means for *multi-system achieving* in this proposed new way of biologically maximizing careers.

PROFIT FROM THE PREDICTABILITY OF THE MAXIMIZING PROCESS

How much more successful would your career and your life be if you could <u>know</u> whether a project was going to fail or succeed before you even began it?

The maximizing process is knowable, predictable, and "harnessable" – not just generically but personally. *This is because the maximum for your system is a constant.* Therefore, maximizing forces will act on your system in consistent and predictable ways. Once you discover how they have supported and opposed your system in your past, you can predict how they will react in the future. You will then know which projects to choose or to avoid to ensure your career success. The provided exercises will support the review of your past: The exercises in the *Sourcing-your-Savant Exercises* in Chapter 7 will support the review of your past.

Historical patterns of events since your childhood will identify, with shocking consistency, the types of projects favored by mechanisms that maximize. It will be no surprise that projects which incite top-talent *flow*, your maximized state, will be favored most. Expect to be catapulted forward by coincidences and flow events. Breakthrough synthesis will increase dramatically. You will have the means to achieve bigger goals more successfully.

This is the simple, consistent, predictable, dynamic order that created our seven iconic innovators. They excelled through a biologically maximized career modus operandi. Just as models and actors know how to position their face in every scene for the best light, our seven achievers learned to unconsciously position themselves for the flow of breakthrough syntheses and coincidences. They capitalized on this predictability to achieve at their maximum.

The more contrary you are to your biological maximum, the more you can expect to be impeded by blocks and negative experiences. The extremes of Steve Jobs' career offer strong examples of when he was and was not biologically compliant.

Our health, and even our patience, is unforgiving when maximization has been experienced and then lost. Thwarted creativity in the field of one's greatest strengths and meaning may turn out to be the key cause of illness in aspiring executives. It is a mistake for the individual and the world to push a career in opposition to the maximizing flow.

EMBRACE THE NEW CAREER MAXIMUMS

Emulate the iconic founders of
Amazon, Apple, Google, Facebook, and Microsoft

Many aspire to the success of our seven super-achievers: Bill Gates (Microsoft), the two Steves: Jobs and Wozniak (Apple), Mark Zuckerberg (Facebook), Larry Page and Sergey Brin (Google), and Jeff Bezos (Amazon). They have achieved the goals that many pursue in their careers. Many mistakenly assume that they accumulated their wealth and acclaim through their pursuit of these rewards directly. Many therefore try to emulate what their pathways seem to have been in order to acquire comparable extrinsic rewards.

The biologically maximized career

However, the formula these seven successful innovators truly share is a biologically maximized career path. It was their pursuit of intrinsic rewards that led to the external manifestation of their internal wealth and success. By operating at their biological maximum, internal and external maximizing mechanisms and processes linked up to enable them to frequently perform beyond their potential. Functionality, growth, and creativity automatically emerged that are not available when we operate as separate entities.

There is an addictive pull to doing meaningful, challenging work to which we are biologically predisposed. Only by harnessing a machinery dedicated to our biological maximum may we know our true career potential. Once you understand the biologically driven career strategy of our seven super-achievers, you realize not only that it is totally replicable in your own life but how to do it.

Serial top-talent flows or serial internal maximizations

Flow state is our maximized state. In *flow* we operate at peak performance and peak growth. We have functionality and capabilities above our norm. However, the *flow* states experienced serially by our super seven had them operating 100% in their savant state.

In top-talent *flow* they applied their strongest most satisfying talents to the work they were biologically predisposed to do and, in fact, biologically addicted to doing. Internal biological incentives enticed them to operate in serial states of top-talent *flow* and the serial breakthrough synthesis that is its byproduct. New functionality perpetually emerged in them with every top-talent *flow* experience. They scaled frontier after frontier in their most meaningful field with world-changing consequences – Google, Amazon, Apple, Microsoft and Facebook.

Serial breakthrough synthesis or serial information creation or serial frontiering™

Years of serial breakthroughs in the territory of their strongest, most rewarding, and most addicting talents yielded their incredible career achievements. This addiction of our seven icons to serial states of top-talent *flow* was compounded by a second biological addiction. This addiction was to the frontiering™ or serial breakthrough synthesis that occurred at the frontiers they were scaling. The cumulative effects of these two benevolent biochemical addictions *pulled* them to advance our world. They were sufficiently compelling that the disciplined linear hard work traditionally promoted for career advancement was never required.

The career success of each of our seven iconic founders is defined by their moments of breakthrough synthesis when they re-mixed the known to create the new. They all had access to *seemingly serendipitous information* that they synthesized into the breakthroughs that peppered their careers. Breakthrough synthesis is evolution's way. Take a page from nature's silver linings playbook. Serial breakthrough synthesis is the modus operandi for a biologically maximized career.

Brilliant breakthroughs for the ungifted?

Is it possible for ordinary people, non-creatives, or the change-adverse to routinely experience effortless epiphanies, brilliant breakthroughs, and fruitful frontiering forays to springboard their careers ahead? The answer is "Yes!" for those who know how to harness nature's maximizing process to source then re-combine existing information systems to create new ones.

You will come to know the indicators of the flow of the maximizing process. Clusters of coincidences are one example. Over time, it will become progressively easier to follow the indicators to be in the right place at the right time for the next piece of information that you need. Even normal intelligence will be able to see how to re-mix to create something new when magical information pieces emerge right in front of you. It will become routine.

- Could it be that the seven iconic super-achievers who founded Google, Amazon, Apple, Microsoft, and Facebook did not need to be as creative, innovative or as brilliant as we might have thought to attain their life-changing and world-changing careers?
- Could it be that they only needed to be able to source and re-combine existing information systems to create new information systems?
- Could it be that our seven were, in fact, expert breakthrough synthesizers?
- Could serial breakthrough synthesis as a way of life have been their shared formula for career success?
- Could it be yours?
- Could you become as world-changing as these icons?

Breakthrough synthesis redefines leading?

Managers manage existing human systems. Leaders penetrate new territory or bring new information systems into existence. The person with the expertise and passion for penetrating unknown territory will always be the leader. The person creating the next iteration of the world will always be the leader. Therefore, breakthrough synthesis will define the leader of the future.

Consequently, our seven iconic executives were leaders even if they never conformed to any of the competencies promoted by the leadership development industry. Those competencies are just window-dressing. Breakthrough synthesis is this essence of leadership. It determines whether you will or will not be the leader.

But there is more. Revisit the definition of breakthrough synthesis for a moment. Is not each person an information system which may be re-combined to create a new information system? Are not all collections of human resources information systems? Could leadership itself then not be better defined in terms of breakthrough synthesis using human information systems? This is obviously a whole other chapter of career maximums best saved for a future article.

8

THE NEW CAREER MAXIMUMS
– Part Two – continued

PART TWO: BORROW EXTERNAL POTENTIAL
External support for your biologically maximized career –
Borrow from nature and surrounding systems: predictability, power, resources, information, functionality, creativity, growth, and frontiering™.

THE SCIENCE BEHIND BREAKTHROUGH SYNTHESIS
- continued

Part One and Part Two contain biological discoveries and theories by the author resulting from extensive executive interviews, examinations, and experimentations which applied scientific method to the lives of individual executives and, especially, multinational executives. This has resulted in a new biologically maximized modus operandi for human beings that bypasses cultural interference.

This new way of operating prescribes full integration into biological mechanisms and processes inside and outside of us which have evolved to work together synergistically but which have been culturally overruled. I have created a link to material that hints at some relevant science to explain in laymen's terms what enables the breakthrough synthesis to work. Hopefully, this brief description will suffice until separate articles may be written with more details about the relevant scientific discoveries. At minimum, it will provide the terminology that those who are interested may research to learn more.

Relevant biological processes

In brief, the following touch on how the maximizing machinery provides the information fuel for the breakthrough synthesis to generate quantum leaps in new information that may define new career highs for you:

1. **Power for the maximizing machinery:** There is an unending dance of systems re-maximizing to a contextual system changed by other systems which in turn were forced to re-maximize when their context was changed by other systems re-maximizing and so on endlessly.

2. **Information source:** The information fuel for new information systems comes from the raiding of information pieces from synergistic systems to enable a system to re-maximize to its changing contextual system. These information pieces are re-combined again using the breakthrough synthesis on which everything in this article relies.

3. **Grouping of information sources:** Spontaneous self-organizing or sudden ordering of the larger contextual system groups us with the best synergy partners from which to source information fuel to re-maximize. This sudden leap to order systems for synergies will improve their mutual chances of survival. Complexity theory is relevant to the re-ordering of this complex contextual system.

4. **Information access:** The information to be re-combined for the breakthroughs appears as coincidences or co-maximizations in one's immediate context or reality. It is the grouping of synergistic systems noted in point 3 that causes clusters of relevant coincidences of information to emerge in one's life. The more one is maximized (in top-talent *flow*, for example) and being orchestrated by the maximizing machinery, the greater the number and value of the coincidences experienced.

5. **Information re-mix – information creation – information quantum leaps:** The process of emergence is behind the breakthrough synthesis. It is what causes information pieces to be re-combined nonlinearly to generate leaps to new wholes which are greater than the sum of their parts. It is the means to adapt to the continuous contextual changes of *the dance*.
A collection of systems is orchestrated by biological spontaneous order or self-organizing principles to pool their resources so that they may each maximize their respective systems for survival. This information re-mix to create new information which will enable systems to adapt is the essence of the work of the maximizing machinery and its component systems of systems.

6. **Goal attainment and problem-solving:** By using the same self-ordering and emergence mechanisms, it is possible to change the information structure of one's personal system so that peripheral elements of your maximizing formula change. This maximizing formula change will then group you with different synergy partners who will share information more relevant to your new goal.

The clusters of coincidences now in your reality will be relevant to your new maximizing formula based on your information structure revised for your new goal. These quantum leaps to sudden knowledge will help you to achieve goals or solve problems by applying the breakthrough synthesis.

Relevant scientific definitions

Self-organization is one of the ideas, models and techniques bundled together as **the sciences of complexity**. It refers to systems that appear to organize themselves without external direction, manipulation, or control. *Self-organization* can be defined as the spontaneous creation of a globally coherent pattern out of local interactions. Self-organizing mechanisms common to biological systems create order from disordered systems using the process of emergence. Self-organized order is a spontaneous pattern from within. It is a product of the generic properties of living matter itself.

Emergence is the way complex systems and patterns arise out of a multitude of simple interactions. In evolutionary theory, emergence is defined as the rise of a system that cannot be predicted or explained from antecedent conditions. A grouping develops properties that none of its members has. The brain is an example of an emergent biological structure. Neither individual neurons nor whole sections of the brain have the properties of a completely integrated brain.

Emergence is the process behind our quantum leaps to sudden insight, sudden knowledge, sudden creativity, creative inspirations, flashes of genius, "Aha!" and "Eureka!" events, intuitive leaps, epiphanies, enlightenment, frontiering, growth, and jumps to whole-brain operation and *flow* states. Emergence is also the same process behind the synergy of co-maximizing systems. *Synergy* is the interaction of multiple elements in a system to produce a combined effect greater and often different than the sum of their separate effects. As such it is a nonlinear process.

Each of us is a living system. Living systems and forces of nature are **nonlinear**. Their outcomes cannot be quantified by *additive* equations. Therefore, cause and effect will not necessarily be functionally related. In linear systems, output is proportional to input. In nonlinear systems, this is not the case. A small input may produce an enormous change in output.

The butterfly effect, popularized by the 2004 science-fiction thriller, is a well-known hypothetical example of **chaos theory** which illustrates how small initial differences may lead to large unforeseen consequences over time. In linear systems change may be predicted by what has happened in the past. In nonlinear systems, change is discontinuous. Progress occurs with sudden unpredictable jumps. Sudden transitions may result from dramatic reorganizations (McClure, 1998*). Our "Aha!" and "Eureka!" events and other results of breakthrough synthesis involve emergence, nonlinear transactions, chaos theory, complexity theory, and sudden self-ordering systems.

A complex system is a system composed of interconnected parts that, as a whole, exhibit properties or behaviors not obvious from the properties of the component parts. This repeats the definition of emergence and the example of the brain. This is also the breakthrough synthesis' information creation process or creativity that drives the continuous re-maximization *dance*. It is this same process that we will be using to drive your career to its maximum.

Please note that I use the term '*quantum leap*' *conceptually* to help you to internalize the required change process. A quantum leap actually uses the process of *emergence*. However, the term '*emergence*' suggests a linear process for what is actually nonlinear. *Emergence* therefore does not help me to ready your system for a leap to change. So, I will call these sought-after career and work breakthrough states 'quantum leaps.'

Do you notice how all of these terms reiterate or add dimensions to the basic breakthrough synthesis that generates the creativity to solve maximization challenges? Imagine harnessing the essential creative force of adaptation and evolution of all living systems to advance your career. Could it be that our seven breakthrough synthesizers who founded Google, Amazon, Apple, Microsoft, and Facebook merely tapped into the creativity of the universe and the way human beings have evolved to operate? Is that the true common thread that they share? *McClure, B. A. (1998). *Putting a New Spin on Groups: The Science of Chaos*. Mahway, NJ: Lawrence Erlbaum Associates.

Exploit maximization-linked coincidences

Coincidences are yet another of the sudden leaps to new knowledge being promoted. They too are products of breakthrough synthesis. A single coincidence has been responsible for some of the most spectacular careers. However, a coincidence is also the information fuel for breakthrough synthesis. Three to seven coincidences or information systems are usually enough for the re-mix to create a significant new information system: an "Aha!" or "Eureka!" event, for example.

Coincidences are both the fuel and the product of breakthrough synthesis. Fortunately, integrating into the maximizing machinery will exponentially explode your experience of coincidences. How delightful! These coincidences, of course, will fuel a plethora of career-making breakthrough syntheses. Your career maximum will increase commensurately. How to cultivate these catalytic coincidences is an article in itself. However, here is a brief introduction.

Officially, **a *coincidence*** is the simultaneous occurrence of events that appear significantly related but have no discernible causal connection. However, the *coincidences* that you will be experiencing with this proposed new career maximizing methodology *will be causally linked to the maximizing process for your system.* These are *maximization-linked* coincidences. Because they will seem serendipitous, the term 'coincidence' still works for our purposes.

However, they are actually *co-maximizations* or synergies among fellow maximizers. Living systems grab information from each other to fuel breakthrough synthesis to generate creative solutions to maximizing or adaptation challenges. The new information systems created by the re-mix appear as the coincidences in your life. However, these created coincidences are also the fuel for the next round of breakthrough syntheses or maximizing. In effect, breakthrough synthesis *is* the maximizing process. It both creates coincidences or information systems and uses them.

Accordingly, a cluster of coincidences will always indicate the flow of the maximizing process in your reality. The closer you are to your maximized state, the more compliant you will be to being orchestrated by the maximizing machinery to the right information at the right time for breakthroughs. The self-ordering nature of the machinery will then group you with the systems best able to provide you with the information you need next. This will increase the volume and quality of the information coincidences that you will experience. Your breakthroughs will increase commensurately.

You may recall from *Part One* that your maximized state is top-talent *flow* or a *flow* state that derives from applying your strongest, most preferred, talents to the field or application that is most meaningful to you. If the coincidences in your life are sparse or nonexistent, then you likely have moved out of the flow of the maximizing process. You are not maximized. You are sitting idly on the riverbank with the other unmaximized living systems. You will have no information fuel for the quantum leaps to career-making breakthroughs, insights, and flashes of genius.

These coincidences are not psychological or RAS events

These *maximization-linked* coincidences are not simply psychologically meaningful events as Jung proposed in his definition of 'synchronicities.' These are not simply psychological transactions whereby you confer meaning on unrelated events. *These are true physical events which result from the shared information pieces from your co-maximizing partners. These 'coincidences' are physical symptoms of the **underlying dynamic order** of a singular process which might be called **'maximizing'** or **'adaptation'** or **'growth'** or **'creativity'** or **'creation'** or **'emergence'** or **'self-ordering'** or **'problem-solving'** or **'breakthrough synthesis.'***

Nor are these *coincidences* or *information quantum leaps* or *co-maximizations* the result of your **reticular activating system (RAS)** seeing whatever you have been focused on. Your RAS is your information filter or gatekeeper. It is the reason why, when you buy the car you have been researching, you will see that model everywhere. It has evolved to filter thousands of items per second to select the information that you need for survival. Your RAS may help you to identify the best coincidences for your next breakthrough synthesis. However, it obviously does not create those coincidences. It is filtering true physical events.

9

SOURCING YOUR SAVANT:
Hyper-Focus your Career on your Genius

Releasing your inner savant requires operating at your maximum. Mechanisms and processes have evolved inside of us and outside which are committed to maximizing living systems for survival.

When one complies with this internal-external '*machinery*' to allow oneself to be maximized, magic happens. The internal links with the external. Circuits inside and out complete. Processes partner. Mechanisms mesh. Systems synergize and synchronize. Synchronicities surge. Coincidences cluster to catapult you to your goals. Results far exceed the linear projection from one's start point. The whole becomes greater than the sum of the parts.

Your internal potential is extended by the external capabilities of both the maximizing machinery and the other systems that it orchestrates. You are able to operate beyond your innate potential. You have sourced your savant (see *The New Career Maximums – Part One*). The exercises in this article are designed to identify your personal formula for operating in your savant state.

We need only examine your past savant moments to generate more of them in your future. Careers have been made through a few flashes of genius. Worlds have been changed. Discover your potential planetary footprint before you dilute it for other life and career priorities.

A biologically maximized career

1. If we removed all restrictions and provided you with every freedom and resource, what could the '*maximized you*' accomplish?
2. What is the work for which you are "biologically predisposed to excel" and "biologically predisposed to crave"?
3. What would your career become if you applied your strongest most rewarding talents on their most meaningful, impactful, and valued application over a lifetime?
4. What would your career become if those talents were to continuously upgrade over your lifetime at your maximum possible growth rate?
5. What could you accomplish if you only focused on the application and growth of your strongest talents over a lifetime?

In *The Secret Career Strategy of the World's Most Successful Executives*, we learned about the biologically maximized career from the seven iconic founders of Amazon, Microsoft, Google Facebook, and Apple: Jeff Bezos, Bill Gates, Larry Page and Sergey Brin, Mark Zuckerberg, and the two Steves, Jobs and Wozniak, respectively.

In *The New Career Maximums* Parts One and Two, we discovered that the careers of these seven super-achievers were peppered with world-changing breakthroughs reflective of savant states. We learned how the compliance of these seven icons to biological maximizing processes led them to *lead* addictive careers of serial breakthroughs, serial frontiering™ or scaling of new frontiers, serial growth, serial creations, serial emotional highs, and serial *flow* states caused by operating at their biological maximum applying their strongest, most rewarding talents to their most meaningful creations.

Their sudden-knowledge leaps included flashes of genius, *"Aha!"* and *"Eureka!"* events, sudden insights, sudden knowledge, sudden creativity, creative inspirations, intuitive leaps, epiphanies, and enlightenment. Even a few of these have made careers life-changing and world-changing. What could your career become with serial breakthroughs? We learned how and why even those of ordinary intelligence may cultivate this *savantism*. Use the unprecedented exercises below to source your inner savant for exceptional work and an exceptional career.

Discover your savant formula

Your maximum state is a constant. Nature's processes and mechanisms for maximizing living systems for survival is also a constant. Therefore, the maximizing machinery will be very consistent as to how it pressures your system to operate at its maximum. Accordingly, it will be predictably consistent as to which projects and work and career goals it will facilitate or thwart. This predictability is harnessable for greater career success and greater lifetime achievement. It gives you the means to garner the support of the maximizing process and the systems under its purview to achieve beyond your potential.

If we know how maximizing forces have pressured your system in the past, we will know how they will pressure your system going forward. You can capitalize on this consistency and predictability. You can predict the future from your past. Imagine knowing in advance that a project will succeed or fail. Predictability enables project and goal selections which will have a greater chance of success. As a corollary, it also means you will not be damaged by choosing projects that will be opposed by the maximizing flow. Let's begin now to examine historically the circumstances around your past peak performances and breakthroughs. We may then develop a savant formula to repeat, accelerate, and amplify exceptional performance in the future.

Examine 12 categories of your past maximums

Let's get down to determining your formula for your biologically maximized career. This exercise is far more powerful than any existing testing for talents or aptitudes. This is because it is about identifying what *nature* considers your biological maximum.

We would therefore expect indicators of support by the maximizing machinery to emerge when you are applying your strongest most gratifying talents to their most meaningful, impactful, and valued application. Your maximum. You would especially achieve your maximum if you were operating at in a peak performance *flow* state that has emerged while you are using and improving those top talents.

In this exercise you will analyze one or more of these twelve categories of events from your recent past, or, if necessary, all the way back to your childhood. This is possible because the formula of *each* of the twelve categories and *all* of the twelve will be consistent over your lifetime. The maximizing machinery is consistent in how it supports and opposes your system because your system has a single maximum and that is its goal state. You will uncover several consistent patterns of events from your past. You are about to discover a level of order in your life that you may not have noticed yet.

WHAT TO LOOK FOR
Indicators of operating at your maximum

The maximizing machinery's sole goal is to maximize you. Anything that will help to accomplish that goal will be supported. Anything contrary to that goal will be opposed or thwarted in an attempt to pressure you into a better direction for survival. You can only merge with the maximizing machinery when you are moving in the direction of your maximum. That is when the magic happens. Circuits otherwise inaccessible will complete. In

The New Career Maximums Part Two, we learned that there are always clusters of coincidences and other information leaps all along the integrated flow of living systems maximizing and re-maximizing to changing contexts.

Your formula or strategy for the future

Therefore, we only need to identify those events from your past where there was breakthrough synthesis inside or outside of you. These events will tell us when you were maximized and integrated into the maximizing flow. When we analyze these events for themes, we will know when the maximizing flow was supporting you and thus when it will support you in the future. We will then be able to develop a formula for you to attain your biologically maximized career. We will have a formula for sourcing your inner savant and getting paid for it.

Serial top-talent flow states

Any events in which you went into *flow* state around the use or improvement of strongest, most rewarding talents - your maximum performance - would be examples of you operating at your biological maximum. They would provide the best indicators of what your formula should be going forward. There will be lots of indicators of being supported by the machinery in this state. Examine those events as a model of what to look for. These top-talent *flow* states will define your biological maximum.

You advance reality: world-changing creativity, creation, upgrades, and innovations

The events you will be studying in your past must all impact, advance, or change reality in some way. You will find that the maximizing indicators will confirm support for 'work' events associated with creativity, innovation, or creation. We are obviously meant to be creative beings participating in the perpetual creative flow of the maximizing machinery that drives nature.

Savant-like *Information leaps inside or outside of you:*

- *serial coincidences* and other facilitators that speed/enhance progress
- *serial breakthroughs:* "*Aha!*" and "*Eureka!*" events, flashes of genius, epiphanies sudden knowledge, sudden insight, intuitive leaps, enlightenment sudden creativity, sudden creation, creative inspirations
- *leaps to emotional highs*

Your top-talent *flow* states or maximized state will be filled with breakthrough leaps such as the above. These leaps belie the creative process that is solving maximizing challenges. This creative process is one of re-combining existing information systems to create new information systems.

This breakthrough synthesis is the essence of nature's creativity. It is how living systems adapt to their environment. It is how they re-maximize once a context has changed. These leaps or breakthrough syntheses or maximizing flow that facilitate survival are what you will be looking for in one or more of the twelve categories of pat evens you are about to analyze. You will be looking for the times that you collided with the breakthrough synthesis of the maximizing machinery for living systems. The machinery or maximizing flow is what orchestrates you to the right information at the right time for the breakthrough or leap.

Savant-like performance leaps and achieving beyond your norm

Events in which we shift into our top-talent *flow* states are also leaps. They are leaps to peak performance and peak growth. They are leaps to altered consciousness. They are leaps to maximization. They are leaps to unification in which theoretically 100% of your body's resources are trained on the activity at hand – an activity that is adaptive for your system.

Serial frontiering™ *into unknown territory*

Obviously, if you attached to nature's breakthrough synthesis, you are going to be continually penetrating new territory. You will therefore want to look at the kinds of territories that you felt comfortable penetrating the unknown in your past. That is your internal system telling you what is natural to you as part of your biological maximum. This is especially true if you are normally fearful of moving into unknown territory.

Serendipitous projects accelerated by maximizing magic

You will be looking for past projects or work that seems to complete as if by magic. These will be events in which the road seems to rise up to meet you. You will be looking for the themes, the commonalities, and the formulas for these events so you can choose your projects and goals to capitalize on them. Again, you want to determine what kind of activities, projects, and goals are supported. You will be looking for the very events that you want to increase in your future.

10

THE TWELVE EVENT-THEMES FOR SOURCING YOUR SAVANT

You are now ready to choose one or more of the below categories to analyze for your best formula for a biologically maximized career which benefits from your savant capabilities. Twelve categories of events are provided below to give you a way to examine times in your past when you successfully partnered with the maximizing flow.

All twelve categories are interchangeable. All twelve patterns of events will point you in the same direction. They are interchangeable. Therefore, "go with the flow." Choose the one(s) which feel easiest for you or provide you with the most information.

Identify past examples of maximizing support

Your personal maximum is a constant. Therefore, the support or opposition of the machinery trying to maximize you is very consistent. Analyze past supported events for commonalities in any of the twelve categories. Maximizing indicators will confirm support for 'work' events in which you use or improve your strongest talents.

Develop formulas and strategies for ways to increase the number and power of such maximized events in the future to achieve breakthroughs and goals beyond your potential. From what you have learned, you should be able to develop the formula for your biologically maximized career.

Nature is surprisingly consistent in its intent to ensure our survival. All twelve categories prove identical support for the use and enhancement of your top talents. Future support may therefore be predicted. It is therefore harnessable. You can look like a psychic without ever being one.

Below is a summary of twelve themes of events to examine in your past so you can capitalize on their recurrence in your future. Discover the surprising consistency for when maximizing mechanisms facilitated or opposed your 'work'-related achievements. Our realities are not as random and chaotic as they may first appear.

1 **Unpaid Work Theme:**
    events of work you crave so much that you would do it for free
2 **Two Knowledge Themes:**
    a) *sudden-knowledge theme*: in what domains do your leaps in sudden knowledge occur?
    b) *knowledge-pursuit theme*: the knowledge you naturally crave
4 **Frontier-Pursuit Theme:**
    events in which you felt compelled to penetrate new unknown territories of growth, learning, creation, and achievement despite fear of the unknown.
5 **Two Creativity/Creation Themes:**
    a) *sudden-creativity theme*: your pattern of leaps to sudden creativity
    b) *creation-pursuit theme*: the creations or creativity you crave or the
        key creative expression of your system
7 **Meaning-Pursuit Theme:**
    the meaningful work or contributions you crave to make
8 **Top-Talent Flow Theme:**
    events where flow state emerged during the application of your strongest most preferred talents.

9 **Projects Theme:**
> projects in which maximizing signs occurred: serial breakthroughs, serial frontiering™, serial top-talent flow events, leaps in knowledge/creativity, positive emotions, coincidences

10 **Core-Expansion Theme:**
> expansions or intensifications of your system around its core strengths thus increasing its impact on reality

11 **Resonance Theme:**
> frequency-sensing events which allowed you to operate in the unknown as if from total knowledge based on frequency sensing.

12 **Positive Emotions:**
> events in which passion, excitement, and enthusiasm emerged during work that impacted reality in some way.

No Themes:
> If you have lived your life directed by external elements (externally referenced) rather than complying with your natural addictive drives internally (internally referenced) you will have less consistent patterns or fewer of them to help you with these life themes exercises.

Choose to learn all twelve categories of events

There is an important reason why you will eventually want to investigate all twelve categories. This is because this will not be a one-time exercise. It will become your new routine modus operandi. You will analyze immediate events as they happen to choose the direction that will keep you hugging the flow of the maximizing process. Repeating the exercise for more current events will be the way you will read, merge into, and capitalize on the maximizing machinery going forward.

These twelve analyses will provide the information that you need for your daily decision-making, goal-setting, and goal achievement. You will know what kind of job choices and careers will not work for you. In addition, models from one category may be more useful for some goals than others. Therefore, the larger your database of historical models from all twelve categories, the more information you will have to draw on to capitalize on the maximizing machinery daily. If you feel as if an event is a maximum model from your past but you cannot figure it out, try looking at it from the perspective of some of the other categories.

Your inventory of past models from all twelve categories will give information for you to move safely and expediently into unknown territory where no other information is available. You will not have to have specific information on the new territory. You will know you are going in the right direction based on the indicators of the maximizing flow.

You know you will be moving with the trends of all of the systems that the maximizing flow is synchronizing and synergizing. You will therefore be part of a dynamic stability. You will be moving *with* your support systems. This will make you a frontiering™ expert with maximum adaptivity and creativity. Try to learn enough from these past events in all twelve categories so that you have the information, power, and ideal direction to succeed at any frontiering™ project you might want to undertake.

Knowing all twelve categories will put you into a better position to apply your greatest talents to make your greatest impact on our world. You will have more information to amass your greatest physical, emotional, and meaning rewards and leave your greatest legacy. And, as a corollary, you will also learn where not to pursue goals. You will have a broader knowledge of what projects will not be supported. You will know what kind of job choices and careers will not work for you. You will know what will cause blocks and negative experiences in your life.

This exercise is not only important for understanding your own system but for capitalizing on any human system you lead to achieve goals. No matter which events clients tell me about I can extrapolate their personal themes backwards or forwards to know what likely occurred in their past and to know how they may more sure-footedly and more impactfully proceed into the future.

Future articles will present new ways to use the historical themes of any human system - a company, country, or humanity – to achieve goals. It will rewrite leadership, leadership development, organizational development, innovation, project management, change management, talent management, and certainly career management. Thus, to repeat, there will be advantages to learning all twelve of these categories or patterns or themes of events.

Test your savant formula hypothesis for predictability

Once you have analyzed your past pattern of events for themes and commonalities, try to develop a prescription or formula for replicating that level of performance in the future. Then test out your hypothesis and adjust it until your results become predictably successful. Test out your formula until the expected indicators of operating at your maximum within the maximizing flow increase dramatically.

Once you have confirmed the reliability of your formula in safe ways using less critical goals, then run your work and your career in compliance with it. Choose goals and projects that will be supported by the maximizing machinery. Compare your results with projects that you know have not been historically supported. How early on in an unsupported project are you able to determine it will not be successful and get out of it?

HYPER-FOCUS YOUR CAREER ON YOUR GENIUS

Some people have a sense since childhood that they are meant to be world-changing. They are meant to advance the world in a meaningful and impactful way. If you are one of these people, this exercise has now given you the means to commit to a career at your biological maximum. It has given you the means to hyper-focus your career on your genius. It has given you the means to follow in the footsteps of our seven iconic founders of Google, Amazon, Microsoft, Facebook, and Apple to create a career which keeps you operating at savant levels around your greatest strengths while continuously improving them.

It has given you your formula for leaving your largest most impactful, most meaningful contribution to the world. It has given you your formula for serial breakthroughs, serial leaps to genius, serial top-talent *flow* states, serial frontiering™, and serial growth in functionality and creations. You have the formula for operating beyond your potential by extending your capabilities with those of nature's maximizing process for the survival of living systems and indeed all of these systems that it synchronizes and synergizes. So now the question to ask yourself is what will your career look like from the age of 85 in a rocking chair when you have grown and created at your maximum?

What will be your legacy? What is the creativity, or the creations, or impact on the world that your greatest talents operating at full power after years of concentrated growth could achieve? If you could leave any legacy from your personal creativity, talents, and invention, what would that look like? If you were going to advance the world with your greatest strengths, what would that look like? Now that you have defined your maximum, it is up to you how much you want to fall short of that maximum for other priorities in your life. What must you achieve to sit satisfied in your rocking chair at age 85?

11

THE UNPAID WORK THEME

Events of doing work for which others would charge that you crave so much you would do for free

These are events relating to work that is so compelling and you do so well that you might even pay for the opportunity to do it. To discover your unpaid work theme, you will want to look at events in your past when you felt compelled to do phenomenal amounts of work motivated only by its intrinsic rewards. The mere joy of doing the work was its own reward. Review experiences in your recent past or your distant past all the way back to childhood where you applied considerable effort to work you were passionate about doing but happily did for free.

Not only were you drawn to do this work, but magic happened whenever you did it. The magic, of course, was the signposts of having merged with the maximizing flow. The addictive qualities of these events derive not only from the addictive drives to use and improve your key talents but from the emotional high, the increased meaning, and draws built-into talent-focused *flow* state. How can you go back to plodding work after all of this magic of coincidences catapulting you forward?

Include in your inventory all those work experiences that you wished you had more opportunities to repeat. Consider, as well, those work events that you wish you could have a job or even a career around doing. Now look for the common thread or generic theme that runs through all of them.

The majority of these events will relate to the application of your strongest talents. If you have been wondering what those top talents are, you will now know. Events in this category identify the core talents and related addictive drives around which your system will be pressured to unify by maximizing forces. These unpaid 'work' events are a demonstration of your system perfectly unified and operating at its maximum.

One of the commonalities of this category of events that you should look for is that they all relate to you changing reality in some way. The impact of this 'work' is registered somehow in the world external to you. The world is different because you have done this 'work.' Given all of the resources and freedom you would wish, this 'work' is what you would love to spend your life doing. This 'work' is the creative expression of the essence of your system.

Select several models from your past to put into your inventory for future reference. Now, develop a formula based on your unpaid work events which will precisely define the kinds of projects that maximizing forces will support in the future. Then any time that you want to experience this kind of support from the maximizing machinery you can choose projects with the same formula as those in your past.

Because unpaid work events are based on addictive drives, we have evolved to maximize us, the more you do this kind of work, the more you will want to do it. Over time you will be compelled to do more and more of this kind of 'play' work.

Also, you will get better at it the more you do it. Your capabilities will be expanding around your core so that your impact on reality increases. Unfortunately, over time you will find that your system grows less tolerant of 'work' work that does not stretch your use of your top talents. Once you get started with your partnership with the maximizing flow, you will not want to go back. Therefore, the only smart career strategy is a biologically maximized one.

You can fight this and force yourself to earn a living contrary to these biological biases. But how much smarter, more desirable, and more meaningful your life would be if your income was from unpaid work of the forms or models of those in your past. You would also be maximized to do your best work and hence earn your best rewards. It is more advantageous *to work with the predictability of the maximizing machinery* than to fight it.

12

KNOWLEDGE-PURSUIT or LEARNING-PURSUIT THEME

Events which identify the theme of knowledge that you are innately driven to pursue. What is the knowledge you naturally crave?

If you had a computer that could give you all of the information that you are truly passionate about knowing, what is the theme of information you would seek? What is the field of that information? Take a look at the times in your past when you exerted great effort to find out new information. Pay particular attention to those events where all of the pressure to discover this new information came from an insatiable drive to know from inside of you.

You will undoubtedly find that your *knowledge-pursuit theme relates to the use and improvement of your top talents*. The same addictive drives motivate both. Therefore, the more you comply with these drives to pursue this specific field of knowledge, the more you will want to give in to them. The more you learn about this subject relating to your top talents, the more you will want to learn. As a result, your knowledge-pursuit theme will be just as compelling as your unpaid work theme. And your success with the discovery of the desired information will have just as much magic attached.

Clusters of information coincidences, flow events, *Aha!* experiences, emotional highs, *flow* states, and synergies will also accompany your pursuit of knowledge in partnership with the maximizing machinery. The *pull*, excitement, and fun of the knowledge-pursuit events will be very different than the *push*, discipline and work that you normally need to do research. You will be able to easily differentiate the category of events that I am talking about for you to put into your inventory. The ones we are interested in are light and thrilling. The other events are heavy, tedious, de-energizing, and have no evidence of support from the maximizing machinery.

The more you use your talent-based knowledge-pursuit addictive drives, the more you will want to use them. Therefore, over time, knowledge pursuit will become faster, easier, more compelling, more exhilarating, more fun, and less work. These territories of knowledge will pull you ahead as if you are magnetized by it. Imagine how much easier university could have been had you chosen your courses based on those territories supported by internal and external maximizing mechanisms. Imagine how much more rewarding financially and emotionally your career could have been if you were constantly pulled to innovate and create new breakthroughs in your innately-compelled field of knowledge.

In other areas of your life, it might take a tremendous amount of discipline and work to achieve the level of throughput and impact that emerges effortlessly in the territories to which you apply your system of top talents. You could do extensive research, reading, investigation, trial and error, and experimentation to support the application of your top talents yet it will be fun and compelling and even thrilling. These are part of maximizing mechanisms inside and outside of us.

If you routinely free yourself to pursue this information you are passionate about knowing, you will begin to see that the maximizing machinery has been pressuring you to build up a *science* around the application of your top talents or *art* to scale new frontiers. The addictive drives underlying your knowledge-pursuit theme also drive most of the other of the twelve themes. Think how they are pulling the frontiering-pursuit theme, the unpaid-work theme, the creation-pursuit theme, and the core-expansion theme, for example. Obviously, all of the addictive drives creating the nucleus in your system are linked and all are promoting the use and improvement of your top talents. The internal and external maximizing mechanisms are part of the same system: 'the internal-external you' or 'the extended you.'

So, if you lived a lifetime honoring your knowledge-pursuit theme, you would be magnetized to learn the next frontier, the next frontier, and the next. And this is also what the maximizing machinery is pressuring. Identify the topic of the frontiers you pursue. Look at the iterations of knowledge-pursuit and creative impact of your top talents on reality. This is the dynamic foundation that I want for each of you to live your life.

13

THE SUDDEN-KNOWLEDGE THEME

Events in which spontaneous knowledge suddenly emerges to support the application of top talents. In what domains do your leaps in sudden knowledge occur?

W hile the knowledge-pursuit theme is the result of addictive drives innate and personalized to each of us, the sudden-knowledge theme is a capability available to everyone. To collect models of this category, recall events in your recent past or all the way back to childhood in which spontaneous knowledge or whole systems of information suddenly downloaded into your head. You suddenly received precisely the information that you needed next for the work that you were doing.

These events likely occurred when you were doing events of your unpaid-work theme, your creation-pursuit theme, or frontiering-pursuit theme. Sudden knowledge dramatically accelerates your rate of progress or magnifies the results you are able to achieve. It is purposeful and relevant to the ways you are advancing reality.

By examining occurrences of sudden knowledge in your past, you can come up with a formula to significantly increase your future experience of sudden knowledge. That formula will likely be the application of your top talents to scale new frontiers of capability and application while partnered with the maximizing flow. Events of sudden knowledge occur when you are complying with any or all of the other themes in partnership with the maximizing flow.

You can ultimately expect to have sudden access to the information you need at the time you need it as you pursue talent-based projects, especially in *flow* state. Interestingly, this is precisely what has been documented for those who have had near-death experiences which reset them to their natural partnered state.

Sudden-knowledge events may be thought of as information coincidences or quantum leaps in your head. Whole systems of information or pieces thereof can emerge in your thinking. Aha! experiences can become routine. They occur in the same way that information coincidences occur outside of you when you are merged with the maximizing flow. This, of course, again demonstrates that internal and external maximizing forces comprise a single system. A single extended 'you.'

While in the past your sudden-knowledge events were likely nature-initiated quantum leaps, there is no reason why you could not orchestrate future sudden-knowledge events through self-initiated quantum leaps. If this is a skill you would like to have, pay close attention to the upcoming chapter about quantum leaps.

As you might imagine, the ability to have spontaneous knowledge or to innovate new information systems will significantly increase your expertise for frontiering™. Sudden knowledge emerges when you have partnered successfully with the master of frontiering™, evolution. Sudden knowledge occurs when existing information systems are combined to create a new information system. This is the underlying dynamic of frontiering™ that is the essence of evolution and creativity. The maximizing machinery is always opportunistically, synergistically, and routinely combining and recombining systems to solve challenges to maximizing systems singly or collectively.

Because the combining of pieces of existing information systems is accomplished by a process called emergence, it is not obvious how the new information came into existence. Emergence is not linear. It creates a whole system that is more than the sum of its parts. It is the dynamic that drives chaos theory. Emergence makes it seem as if there has been magic or miracles at work. Rather, it is routine if you follow your personal formula for generating them – a formula which you will discover by examining your own past sudden-knowledge events to identify the shared elements.

As you inventory your sudden-knowledge events, check for subject matter themes. Are there more occurrences when you are pursuing your knowledge-pursuit or creativity-pursuit or unpaid-work themes? Did your sudden knowledge multiply and magnify while you were in talent-focused *flow* state?

Is there a particular field in which your more significant events occurred? Were you frontiering™ new territory around your top talents? Were there three to seven information coincidences in your reality just before you experienced a flash of sudden knowledge? This would mean again that what was going on in your head was a part of process that was going on in the other half of your system embedded in your external maximizing machinery. The information from the information coincidences was combined in your head to create new information. This was what caused you to experience a sudden-knowledge event.

14

THE FRONTIER-PURSUIT THEME

Events in which you felt compelled to penetrate new unknown territories of growth, learning, creation, and achievement despite fear of the unknown

This is another category of events resulting from addictive drives internally. This time they relate to our addiction to new frontiers – to new unknown territories for growth, learning, achieving, creating, new functionality, and performance. The pattern of events for you to analyze to discover a theme or formula consists of those times in which you felt yourself pulled by addictive drives to go into new unknown territory even though you are normally resistant to the unknown.

You are not alone. Most people are fearful of venturing into the unknown. However, you are likely to discover something surprising when you investigate frontiering events from your past. You will likely find that there will be one generic territory where you are not only less fearful of the unknown, but you are excited by it. You are enticed by it. You are exhilarated by it.

You will take a chance to *frontier* in this field. As with the other themes, that field relates to the application and improvement of your top talents to scale the new frontiers. The pull of the talent-related addictive drives overrides your usual fear of the unknown. In no time we become pioneers in the territories around our top talents. We become innovators, creators, and knowledge-pursuit addicts.

You will likely find that your progress in this one territory is supported and accelerated by the signposts of partnering with the maximizing flow. Between addictive drives internally and 'drives' externally, even ordinary people can become able to scale new frontiers to advance the field around your key talents. You may find your own performance becomes stellar.

The maximizing machinery consists of perpetual frontiering™. Since we have evolved to be its partner, we have addictive drives which compel us to move into new territory or improve our skills. Because these frontiering drives are addictive drives, the more you use them the more you will want to use them. The more you frontier, the more you will want to frontier. Your courage and boldness, audacity, daringness, and fearlessness will increase with each frontiering experience.

Over time, frontiering skills developed around your key talents will find application in other territories of your life. Therefore, for this exercise, it is important to differentiate the original talent-based frontiering events that are truly part of your frontiering-pursuit theme from your secondary frontiering events. The latter are an application of your frontiering expertise rather than a pursuit of new frontiers compelled by your addictive drives.

As you partner with the maximizing flow, the signposts will guide you to safely and quickly scale new frontiers. The signposts provide information where there is none that you can trust to guide you through the unknown.

Now that you know to look for the maximizing flow, examine successful ventures into unknown territory in your past to provide you with expertise for the future. Add this new information to your formula for the future peak performance. Eventually your frontiering skills will be available for use in every territory of your life, not just with the application of your key talents. You will become the frontiering™ expert this book is designed to help you to become.

15

THE SUDDEN-CREATIVITY THEME

Events in which spontaneous creativity, creative inspiration, or Aha! experiences emerged as an original solution to support the application of one's top talents to creation work that will transform or advance the world in some unprecedented way.

S udden-creativity events are a subtle enhancement to the sudden-knowledge theme. They too relate to experiencing information coincidences in your head. They too are nature-initiated quantum leaps that have been included as signposts of the maximizing flow. They differ in that the sudden creativity is only about the creation of new, original, and unprecedented information. Creativity recombines existing information coincidences or systems to create new information systems that have never existed before. We have named this *breakthrough synthesis* in other articles of the *Biologically Maximized Career* series.

Sudden-creativity events bring something new into existence. They involve new creations that are the product of creativity and innovation. Reality, the world, or the contextual system will be changed in some way during sudden-creativity events. This type of information coincidence is more visibly impactful on reality than sudden-knowledge coincidences which are internal.

16

CREATION-PURSUIT THEME

Events of creativity which you felt compelled to pursue to impact or advance reality. There is likely a territory or theme of creative impact that is addictive for you. *Alternative names: creativity-pursuit theme or creative-expression theme*

With the knowledge-pursuit theme, we examined events compelled by addictive drives related to our strongest talents and capabilities. Creation-pursuit events are similarly motivated. Whereas previously we looked at what your system innately wants to learn, in this exercise *we analyze what your system innately wants to create*, given every resource and every freedom. Knowledge-pursuit events change you inside. Creation-pursuit events change reality outside. Knowledge-pursuit events provide the fuel for creation-pursuit events.

All of us do not seek to be creative in general. Rather, there is a specific territory where it is meaningful for us to change reality or advance the world. Innately, we are biologically predisposed to want to create or impact reality in that particular territory or specific way. In your recent past or all the way back to your childhood, review the events around your greatest creations:

How are you drawn to change reality; to create; to invent; to come up with something new; to produce something; to bring something new into existence?

1. What are the characteristics that are common to all of these times when you were driven to creativity or creations?
2. What is the theme?

3. What would be your formula to increase the quality, quantity and impactfulness of your future creations?

4. What would be your formula for you to leave your greatest legacy to advance our world given unlimited freedom and resources?

5. What is your formula for the improving your performance and your achievements for the future?

6. What will be your personal formula for success and for your life based on the 'partnered you' or the 'internal-external you'?

7. What projects, jobs and career should you choose so that

   - you are always amplified by the maximizing machinery: sudden-knowledge, sudden-creativity, synergies, knowing the ideal directions into the unknown, top-talent *flow* states, and so on;

   - you are compelled by the addictive drives behind your creativity/knowledge pursuit themes to do your fastest work, your greatest work, your most effortless work, and your most meaningfully impactful work; and

   - you operate at peak performance - in top-talent *flow* states - using your greatest strengths while experiencing addictive emotional highs.

This is the prescription for you to experience your greatest rewards internally and externally. This is your formula for your biologically maximized career.

Another way to get at this central core or your *creative-expression theme* is to think of the times you were using your strongest talents with passion, excitement, and enthusiasm. You were totally inflamed, totally motivated to do particular tasks, or totally motivated to do a particular task in some particular way. You were compelled by the addictiveness of top-talent *flow* state.

You are looking for events in which these kinds of positive emotions occurred while you were advancing reality in some way. You were creating in top-talent *flow* state, your most positive emotional state. Your creations felt as if they were expressions of your natural core, your essence. These events will be demonstrating your creativity-pursuit theme, your creation-pursuit theme, or your creative-expression theme. Your creativity-pursuit theme and your positive-emotions theme are linked to each other and to your top talents.

The only negative emotions you might discover with your past events associated with your creativity-pursuit category, if we would refer to them in that way, relate to creative tension. This is a little bit of frustration you experience as you are trying to figure out how to scale the next frontier. The task at hand has to be a stretch in order to pull you into top-talent *flow* state. That is the entrance fee for that benevolently addictive state that has evolved to keep the human species maximizing and adapting.

17

THE MEANING-PURSUIT THEME

Events in which you felt compelled to do work or make contributions motivated by meaning. This work seeks to create something valued by others.

We want to look only at the historical pattern of top-talent meaning-pursuit events around which the machinery has been maximizing you. That means signposts of maximizing such as clusters of coincidences will surround these events. The meaning events to be identified and analyzed from your past are not related to charitable giving. *Your gifts of money or resources should be excluded from your evaluation.* We are instead looking for natural outpourings from your system that addictive drives compel you to do which you hope or wish will be valued by the world.

1. What is innately meaningful as a creative expression of your system?

2. What does this tell you about the theme of the work you are drawn to do or the territory where you most want to benefit the world?

3. What 'work' – using your knowledge-pursuit theme, frontier-pursuit theme, and creativity-pursuit theme – would give your life the greatest meaning?

4. What 'work' would give the most pride in your achievements over a lifetime of pursuing them? When you answer this question you are likely talking about your natural core and your system of strongest talents. Your essence. The foundation of your system.

5. What would be your greatest legacy or the highest most meaningful life work you can envision?

Look back over your lifetime to examine the pattern of events of meaningful work that you have done. Do you see the theme? Do you see where you would like to make your greatest contribution to the world given unlimited time, freedom, and resources?

These events will tell you where your addictive drives, strongest talents, and passions are trying to pull you. These should simultaneously be events where clusters of coincidences and natural quantum leaps will abound to show that you have successfully partnered with the maximizing flow. Your internal-external system is operating fully.

18

THE THEME OF TOP-TALENT *FLOW* STATES

Events where *flow* state emerged during the application of your strongest most rewarding talents

low is the addictive dynamic that we have evolved to keep the species evolving, adapting, and surviving. It is a peak-performance and peak-growth state. As an addicting state of being or altered consciousness, the more you experience *Flow*, the more you want to experience it. The admission price to enter this wonderful emotionally gratifying state is to be stretched beyond your existing capabilities. Therefore, *flow* events perpetually advance us.

Top-talent *flow* is a special subset of this state of being. It emerges as a result of using and improving one's greatest talents to do 'work' that one is biologically predisposed to pursue. It is the most meaningful, valued, and gratifying work. Only components within you that are required for the task at hand are activated. Peak performance results from the singular focus of all of the body's resources on the task at hand. Each top-talent *flow* state results in increasing functionality, upgraded potential, expanding consciousness, and improving cognitive abilities.

Examine your inventory of *flow* events over your lifetime. Omit the ordinary *flow* states which emerged while you were doing chores or sports, for example. Instead, select events in which *flow* state spontaneously emerged while you were applying your greatest talents to make a mark on the world. In other words, select only those events in which you experienced top-talent *flow* state while doing compelling work that you were passionate about and which changed reality in some way, or had a physical manifestation outside of you, or left a footprint on the world.

Especially inventory those times in which you slipped into top-talent *flow* state while scaling a new frontier, penetrating new territory, or invented or created something new. These themes of top-talent *flow* events should be a strong indicator of the true creative expression of the core essence of your system. The will indicate what the maximizing machinery considers your peak or maximum state. They will identify what nature considers to be your greatest strengths or strongest talents.

The addictive drives underlying your top-talent *flow* events will include and integrate with your creation-pursuit, knowledge-pursuit, frontier-pursuit, and unpaid-work drives. They should all link up into the single process that they are. You will know each theme by any other theme. Hence each individually and collectively allows you to predict projects and goals that will be supported in the future. They are interchangeable because they are consistent with the single maximum state of your system.

Coincidences, flashes of genius, and other facilitating events that indicate you are merged with the maximizing flow will increase with any one of them. Top-talent *flow* state is your maximized state. It is the state we are being pressured to attain and sustain by the maximizing machinery. It is our goal state. You will want to remember all of the attributes common to your experiences of top-talent *flow* in your past to help you replicate them in your future. Develop your formula for getting into top-talent *flow* state. If you choose all your major goals to comply with this formula, the 'internal-external you' will be operating at your maximum to achieve them. You will be able to achieve beyond your potential.

19

THE PROJECTS THEME

Projects with lots of signposts of support from the maximizing machinery projects in which maximizing signs occurred: serial breakthroughs, serial frontiering™, serial top-talent *flow* events, leaps in knowledge/creativity, positive emotions, coincidences

Discover the projects supported by the maximizing machinery

The historical projects for you to analyze for themes differ from those examined for the unpaid-work, frontier-pursuit, knowledge-pursuit, creation-pursuit, or core-expansion themes. Those were events and projects which you were internally compelled to do by addictive drives associated with the use and improvement of the top talents. Those drives are part of the internal maximizing process used to maximize you for survival.

The past events to be analyzed for this exercise are those in which you either chose or were given a project or goal which was not based on the other themes. These are projects which are independent of the use and improvement of your top talents. Nonetheless, these projects have all of the signposts indicative of support by the maximizing machinery such as coincidences and breakthroughs.

What we can learn from these successful past projects is how to harness the machinery to ensure the success of future projects. You want to learn how to drive the whole machinery to accelerate and amplify your project's success beyond your innate potential. You want to see how to cultivate coincidences, conscript resources, appropriate assets and capabilities from surrounding systems, and channel the energy and directions of the evolutionary engine to make your future projects even more successful.

Ensure more successful future projects

Now that you know the other eleven themes, you can observe them in action on successful projects in your past.

1. How did the themes play out?
2. What projects worked for you and which ones failed?
3. What did the machinery do to make them succeed or fail?
4. Look at when the projects went off the path. Could you now prevent this in the future?
5. When did they accelerate? When did they slow or stop?

Examine what is happening inside of you and outside to identify signals for potentially successful projects effectively partnered with the maximizing flow.

This inventory of past projects will help you to choose future projects more effectively, ride out their accelerations, shorten or circumvent their blocks more quickly, correct de-railings more proficiently, and avoid crash-and-burn events entirely.

Learn how to repackage and redirect any project to harness the machinery. Learn how to reposition projects to trigger your internal addictive drives to pull you forward. This will change work to fun, engage your greatest functionality, and enable you to operate in peak performance *flow* state as a way of life.

Now that you know what to look for, your past project experience can teach you how to capitalize on your full internal-external system going forward. Once you understand how to do this for your own system, you can apply the same analysis and methods for any human system. You can apply the same approach to corporate systems based on the historical evidence and core strengths of the key players in and around the project. How profitable would a company become if every project it undertook was successful in a big way?

Improve project implementation

If you begin a project and experience no facilitating events, and worse, negative emotions, blocks to your progress and other deterrents, you would have to conclude that this project not going to be supported by the maximizing machinery inside and outside of you. The results will be predicable if you proceed. Even if you push through all of the blocks to get to the end of the project, project goals may still not be met.

For example, it may be discovered the goals were wrong, the goals could not be met by the project, the goals were met by some other project first, or the goals are no longer needed. This is information that the maximizing machinery has that we do not. However, we can operate as if we have that information by analyzing the signposts of the maximizing flow.

There is a reason why the flow was not supporting the project. It was not arbitrary. As you develop your partnership with evolution's machinery, you may come to know those reasons. It could be a) the wrong time, b) the wrong project for you, c) out of sync with the flow and trends around you, d) an alternative route is better, or e) danger, and f) the possibility of damage to your system, to name a few. You will need to make revisions to the project until the symptomatic facilitating events emerge to signal support from the maximizing machinery.

From your analysis of past partnered projects, you will come to know the early feel of projects to pursue and those to avoid. You will come to know your own personal indicators of a potentially successful project. There will be a distinct emotional high, a pull, and a knowingness when you are pursuing a potentially partnered project. There will be a distinct drain in energy and an absence of compelling emotions when you are pursuing an unsupported project. Examining your personal historical evidence will give you an inventory of indicators that you can draw on in the future.

As you learn how to cultivate coincidences, you can even set up you projects to factor them in to your schedule. As you become experienced with generating coincidences, you can build earlier deadlines into your projects. You will know how you can get bigger and better results than you planned on. You can let your projects move nonlinearly with coincidences and nature-initiated or self-initiated quantum leaps.

Improve project selection

Analysis of this category of past events will help you to better choose the projects and goals which will be supported by the maximizing machinery going forward. You will know that you can choose projects which will allow you to achieve goals far bigger than the potential of your system would suggest are possible. The same process applies to all human systems – individuals, companies, countries or humanity as a whole.

20

THE GROWTH OR CORE-EXPANSION THEME

Events of expansions or intensifications of your system around its core strengths to achieve greater impact on reality

The pressure to maximize your system promotes a nonlinear growth path. It pressures you to expand and intensify around the greatest strengths of your system. It pressures you to expand your core strengths by concentric spheres. As the core expands and strengthens, so does its impact on reality.

Maximizing will always honor the core integrity of a living system. From the perspective of maximization, growth is a nonlinear increase, magnification, expansion, intensification or amplification of the core strength of the system rather than a linear progression from form A to form B.

The basic configuration of the system remains the same. Therefore, a human system is maximized around the same core strengths in precisely the same way over its lifetime. It is maximized around its strongest talents and their associated addictive drives that promote their use. There is only one system maximum. The pressures and directions of the maximizing machinery therefore remain constant.

The way they have acted on your system in the past will persist into the future. There is tremendous power in this predictability. Also, you will know what nature considers your strongest capabilities and your natural growth path. You know the direction of your supported creations and how they will increase over time. These will become the formula for your biologically maximized career path.

21

THE RESONANCE THEME

Events where your system resonated with subjects, objects, or activities which proved advantageous. Frequency-sensing events which allowed you to operate in the unknown as if from total knowledge based on frequency sensing.

This is another category of events that may not be useful for examination by novices. Resonance is not intuition or gut-feel. It is frequency-sensing capability that is an advance of what is known so far in dolphins, porpoises, whales, and bats. It goes beyond echolocation. It is a capability that will be increasing within the human species. If you can recall high school physics, tuning forks are used to explore frequency. A common experiment is to use two tuning forks with the same frequency. If one tuning fork is struck, the other will begin to vibrate in sympathy with the first tuning fork to produce the same tone.

Resonance is experienced when you focus on an activity or item relevant to the 'maximized you' that the maximizing machinery favors. Just as with coincidences and sudden knowledge or creativity, resonance is a signpost which will help you to identify and join into the flow of synergistically maximizing and adapting living systems. Resonance is an indicator of something being on your current need to maximize.

If you imagine yourself to be the first tuning fork, you will feel the surge of energy that you would expect when the second tuning fork begins to resonate. For example, look down your to-do list. The item to select as your next activity is the one which invokes the greatest frequency surge as if the second tuning fork is joining the tone of the first. This is the signal that maximizing mechanisms favor this activity from their superior knowledge of all of the living systems which are being synergistically.

By using resonance, you can operate as if you have all of the same information that nature does. Resonance is a phenomenal tool for frontiering™ into new unknown territory. It may take some experimentation to build a relationship with your resonance. However, it is well worth it. What parent would not want their child to have this means to remain safe?

Resonance suits those people who do not like to do a lot of analysis yet want to be able to proceed at top speed in total compliance with the maximizing flow. There are no words or information associated with operating by resonance. You simply operate consistent with the frequency shifts or surges that suggest a second tuning fork is resonating with whatever you are focusing on.

22

POSITIVE-EMOTIONS THEME

Events in which passion, excitement, and enthusiasm emerged during work that changed reality

As with all twelve categories, these are events which will identify your top talents and the way the maximizing forces for living systems have opposed or supported your system in the past. Events in any of the twelve categories will generate positive emotions. This is as you would expect. Positive emotions are one of the signposts of successfully complying with the flow of maximizing systems.

The events from your past to be inventoried in this category are those in which positive emotions are experienced while doing work that will advance reality in some way. These events should be analyzed for commonalities so that formulas may be formulated for replicating them in the future. Analyzing the emotional feel of the events that historically generated positive emotions will allow you to replicate such events in the future. The potential for improvements to your quality of life are substantial.

Determine the *emotional signature* you experienced as you were on your way to what turned out to be a successful outcome. You may use this signature in the future to determine if you are on a successful path. You will want to know the *emotional harmonic* that occurs when you are using your system of key talents, especially in top-talent *flow*. It will become one of the many new information sources or signposts that these twelve themes are identifying for you.

This emotional signature or harmonic will be a tell-tale sign that you are taking the right next steps in partnership with the maximizing flow. It can be used to allow you to frontier quickly and safely through unknown territory. You will even be able to us this emotional harmonic at the beginning of activities and projects to confirm that they are right for you before you commit to them. Your theme of positive emotions can be a predictor of your career success.

23

NO THEMES FOUND

If you have lived your life directed by external elements (externally referenced) rather than complying with your natural addictive drives internally (internally referenced) you will have less consistent patterns and fewer of them to help develop formulas for the future.

Whathat do you do if you cannot see any past patterns or themes of events for any of these twelve categories? What if you see no evidence of past partnering with the evolutionary machinery? What if you find no evidence of operating your complete internal-external system? Not to worry. This is fixable.

Sometimes people must or choose to live externally referenced and created by their realities rather than internally referenced and creating their realities. They have been living their lives responding to the unnatural demands of others or their environments.

There could be financial, cultural, religious, familial, or physical demands that have made them overrule their internal addictive drives. They may have chosen to discipline themselves to follow some formula for success they believe in. They may have been overruling those internal guidance systems to serve external rules.

In short, they may have ignored or overruled the natural drives to which we now want each of you to respond. As a result, they may not have enough examples of having partnered with the evolutionary machinery from which to determine formulas for harnessing its capabilities for future goals. They may have less consistent patterns or fewer of them from which to deduce themes or commonalities. They may have fewer experiences of clusters of coincidences and the other facilitating elements of the maximizing machinery.

The more you comply with the maximizing flow going forward, the more patterns you will see. As soon as you begin partnering with the maximizing machinery as prescribed, the clusters of coincidences and flow events will emerge and you will have the models you need for future reference.

Everyone is going to be testing their hypotheses as to formulas for harnessing the flow on an ongoing basis. You can do the same. Everyone will make corrections as needed based on the response of the maximizing machinery. You will do the same until you can get predictable support from the machinery to achieve your goals more quickly, easily, and expansively. Be patient with the process. Just as those addictive drives associated with our top talents strengthen every time you use them, they also atrophy every time you overrule them. It may take a few trials in order to kick-start your addictive drives again.

24

JOB SEARCH BEFORE ONE IS BIOLOGICALLY MAXIMIZED

The need for proactive serial job replacement in all career strategy

Today's job search strategies seem to have been developed by non-executives and inflicted on executives by an industry committed to promoting them despite their historical failure. How can 1-2 years of daily damage and devaluing for executives to sell themselves into a new job signify success?

Job replacement used to be a career exception. Serial job replacement is now the rule. If we can accept that reality, we can stop trying to apply patches to the inefficiencies and damages inherent in today's job search protocol. It is time for a total re-write. Proactive serial job replacement needs to be fully integrated into all career management strategy.

I have dedicated decades to executive career maximization. I have known many executives before and after job search. I used to be able to just pick up the pieces of the battle-worn job searcher once they returned to employment where my invoices were again covered. Unfortunately, I reached a tipping point.

The destruction of an executive's *esprit de corps* during job search is too heart-wrenching. There is too much loss on every side. Some never recover either their former glory or their former performance levels. Some are never able to reinstate their previous quality of life personally or professionally. Too many are permanently scarred. I felt compelled to create a new less damaging and more efficient job search protocol.

Putting aside the personal devastation for each executive for a moment, it seems to me that this is no way to run the planet. How does it make sense to have your best and your brightest out of commission for a couple of years? Or irreparably damaged, for that matter? These are our world-changers. We need them doing what they do, not destroyed by a job search seeking the opportunity to do what they do. If you were running the world the way you run your company, maximizing your human resources is management 101. Downtime of our leaders is a waste of key human assets.

In addition, the economy and the career needs of individuals are increasing the number of jobs if not careers that we have over a lifetime. Clearly, we need improvements in the efficiency, effectiveness, and humanity of our job search protocol. It is time to stop tweaking the make-shift protocol that was designed decades ago to address the occasional need for job search. What was the exception is now the rule for the majority? We must now accept serial job replacement as a career constant.

Consequently, we must now formally invent an appropriate job search protocol that is fully integrated into life-time career management strategies. We need to make serial job replacement workable, rewarding, purposeful, and profitable. Ideally, we need a method of serial job replacement which is high-growth, high-speed, and nourishing and fulfilling in and of itself. We need a paradigm shift in job search protocols.

25

A BIOLOGICALLY MAXIMIZED JOB SEARCH

The paradigm shift into the biologically maximized career introduced in my previous posts, gave me a completely novel context from which to recommend job search strategy. What would a biologically maximized job search look like for executives? But wait. Biological maximization is holistic. There would not be the need for a separate job search process. It would already be integrated.

Job losses or leaps would simply be part of neutral system corrections to improve system maximization or to solve maximization challenges. Therefore, they could be foreseeable. They could be capitalized upon as with all partnering with the maximizing machinery. What could these neutral system corrections be used for? Quantum leaps in growth? Repositioning for greater performance? Wealth creation? Could it be that we could not just protect ourselves from the damage of today's job search but become so good at serial job replacement that it could be proactively used for profit and gain?

I therefore sought to create a high-growth, high-speed, job search process that actually accelerated executive careers and the growth of their baseline functionality. This became so exciting and successful that I gradually began to build proactive job replacement into my career maximization strategies. Soon every client employment contract was negotiated to maximize the benefits of a new serial job replacement process. Serial severance packages and signing bonuses became a pivotal wealth-creation tool and a signature of my executive career partnering services.

This was indeed excellent lemonade from what had previously been a serious career lemon. However, one must be very good at job creation or job replacement before one may partake of this lemonade. I will need to provide extensive instructions to help you to make this paradigm shift with serial job replacement proficiency.

Therefore, I have broken these instructions up into a number of articles. This first article merely gives us a common understanding of today's executive job search and indicates some of its inefficiencies and damaging aspects. The next article provides a comparison of today's executive job search with that of the new biologically maximizing paradigm. Articles beyond that will start to get more practical to help those wanting to apply the new model. Let's get started.

26

TODAY'S EXECUTIVE JOB SEARCH STRATEGY

Today's job search strategies seem to be based on the sales approaches of the insurance industry developed sixty years ago. Cold-calling and relationship-building techniques that are used to build entire insurance-agent careers are applied to a small job-search project. The same amount of time and effort required to develop a network to launch the lifetime career of a real estate, insurance or executive search agent must be applied to develop a network for a single job search project.

With this much front-end effort, the ROI will therefore be considerably less for this job search project. This is especially the case when neither the development of the skills nor the end products are likely to be more than nice-to-haves when one returns to one's real career. Obviously, today's job search protocol is massively inefficient.

In addition, today's job search industry appears to have grown up around administrative staff and well-meaning counselors. It emerged to protect firing employers with deep pockets. There were few executives or strategists developing the field or taking into consideration how executives operate. So again, it is not been designed for efficiency for the executive target market.

The average job seeker may find a new job in six to seven months. Executives, however, may take one to two years. U.S. Department of Labor statistics suggest job search duration may increase one month for each $10,000 in desired income. Therefore, an executive making $150,000 would be expected to be in job search around fifteen months.

Imagine whom you might become in a year of fear, devaluing, humiliation, and most importantly, not doing meaningful work. As I have alluded in a previous article with respect to Steve Jobs, *"the blocking of creative expression may be the greatest cause of illness in [high-achieving] executives."* I do not like to even have my executive clients retire without some channel for the application of their strongest talents to meaningful work for the audience or context that will value it most.

Only about 15-20% of jobs are advertised on internet job banks and in other publications. Responding to job advertisements is not a good use of executive time and talent. Many are ill-equipped for the technical savvy and menial repetitive work required to pursue advertised jobs. Not only may this approach dampen their spirits, but it may damage their stature in their work communities. Again, we are seeing the flaws of what has evolved as job search protocol. These flaws likely would have been avoided if a protocol had been specifically designed for executives.

The Hidden Job Market

The hidden job market accounts for perhaps 80-85% of all executive hires. Therefore, this should be a key target of any re-written job search protocol. These are positions that are filled before they are advertised and may not even involve the Human Resources department. The hiring manager makes the decision.

Perhaps s/he has an idea for growing the organization and seeks a prospective employee through her/his network. Perhaps someone has quit unexpectedly creating a gap that must be filled immediately. Or the company might have landed a major new client and needs to hire immediately. There may be neither time nor money for either advertising the job or working through a recruiter.

Positions may also be created for candidates who come to an employer's attention through employee recommendations, referrals from trusted associates, direct inquiries, and the networking efforts of a job seeker. Therefore, contacting companies and their respective line decision-makers is a great way to gain inroads and initiate discussions that lead to interviews. Any effective executive job search campaign should focus 80-100% of its time, resources, and strategy to addressing this hidden job market. An opportunity-seeking mindset is therefore an asset. Proposing a project may create the job for which you are hired. Job creation then should be a key part of the job-search-protocol redesign.

Networking or *'stockpiling people'* for information and referrals

The most touted strategy for looking for work in the 'hidden job market' is *networking*. This is a marketing campaign where employers are the buyers, and you are the product. *Cold marketing* means that you apply to employers who do not know you. Thus, you are "going in cold." *Warm marketing* engages an intermediary known to the employer to introduce and vouchsafe for you. As a result, you receive a "warm welcome" instead of a cooler reception.

A lot of focus must be paid to defining the job you are seeking. Next you research to find potential contacts associated with those companies. And finally, you need to have a strategy for getting to those contacts either for the job directly or to refer you or, at minimum, to join your network. It is then ideal to have a customized resumé for each of those approaches.

Given the greater success of warm marketing referrals over cold calling, a networking strategy is promoted. Networking is a way of leveraging the people you already know to get introduced to decision makers at employers you would consider working for. When done with finesse, you are not asking your network contacts for a job. Rather, you are *seeking information that may lead to a job.*

Networking is about building and maintaining relationships with the people around us. Theoretically, the more people you know, the more people that the people you know are connected with, and the more relevant they are, the more powerful your network. Job-hunting is now billed as a contact sport. And networking is obviously a numbers game.

As an information source, networking is pretty inefficient. As suggested above, your ROI is going to be extremely low for the efforts invested to find, attract, and maintain the people in your network. This will need to be addressed in any new job search protocol. It would be more efficient to be able to access the right information at the right time rather than *stockpiling people* on the off-chance that they discover information that may help you with your job search.

Damage and dangers from job search networking

The most successful executives and managers are great networkers. Unfortunately, many executive job seekers who use their work network for job search destroy the very relationships they need to actually do their new job once they get it. Executives need a certain stature to operate at this most senior level. Using their work network from their weakened state or stature as a job hunter may change how they are perceived by their network and, worse, how they perceive themselves.

Personal power is critical at executive levels and one may not recover either inside of oneself or outside with one's network if you use your work network for your job search. For example, if you have always been the magnanimous feeder of your network, asking for job-search favors outside of your usual protocol may make relationships awkward and reveal that relationships are limited to the existing protocol or formula or are not reciprocal. Your relationships may not have the ability to adapt to a new formulation and the old channel is destroyed while you find this out.

My advice is to refrain from beating yourself up for not networking to find your desired job. If you normally have good throughput, then you are likely not procrastinating when you avoid networking. You are sensing real danger in pursuing this highly promoted job search strategy.

Historically, how many times did overruling this resistance to action work out for you? I suspect that it never did. I trust your gut! To back it up, use the *Sourcing Your Savant* exercise criteria to make a rational unemotional decision based on the historical evidence. Remember, the job search industry began with counselors, administrative personnel, career managers, HR people, and executive search consultants. Not an executive among them. Trust your instincts and your history. Operate from your strengths and your maximized state.

Give-to-get networking

There must be mutual gain in networking. Many executives have delicately balanced *quid-pro-quo* relationships in business. This is how business has traditionally been done. There may be permanent repercussions from seeking help from individuals in your work network. "Friends" in your last job may be competitively threatened personally or for their companies by placing you back into a powerful position.

Putting friendship aside, it may be a savvy business strategy for them to keep you from getting into a power position which may diminish their company's profits. Unfortunately, they may proactively pursue that strategy using their own work network to block your job search. Your losses will be compounded if their work network is the same as yours.

However, your vendor networks may want exactly the opposite. If you are likely to use a new job to bring them business, they will happily flex their executive muscle to put you into a position of power with one of their customers. Many large vendors may even have the power and influence to have a current incumbent removed to create a vacancy for you. At minimum, they may offer you an office and resources on their premises for your job search because it is in their interest to do so. But understand, *quid pro quo* will be expected or there may be negative repercussions when you are re-employed.

Hopefully, the new job search design will not only circumvent the inefficiencies but the dangers of networking. It would be ideal to formalize more direct sources of information into the new job-search-protocol redesign. There are also a lot of undesirable menial and administrative tasks inherent in both networking itself and addressing the hidden job market. These need to be eliminated or minimized in the new design.

Executive job search networks and job search work teams

Support networks of fellow job seekers may be good for many. I therefore differentiate them from both your network which supports your work and your main job search network where you are asking contacts for referrals, job information, or jobs. These are pay-it-forward organizations where support and shared information are encouraged from peers in transition.

The intent is that job openings are shared and warm introductions of fellow members to potential employers are encouraged. However, I think the real value is in the shared experience, shared learning, inspiration, and emotional support. For the duration of your job search, these are your peers and colleagues. This is a very different network which deserves cultivation. Below are some examples:

- HAPPEN Canada's largest networking group for executives in career transition
- The Executive Network Group of Greater Chicago
- Exec-U-Net

- Executives Network
- Senior Executive Networking Group: New England
- Technology Executives Networking Group
- Technology Leaders Association
- Kettering Executive Network

Psychological counseling for employer damage control:
The dangers of letting someone inside your head

Psychological counseling harks back to the origins of job search support where employers needed de-hires defused of the emotions which would cause them to initiate legal cases against them. The laws have changed to make this less of a threat. However, the inclusion of psychological practice persists.

Most executives know who they are and their strengths and weaknesses. They will resiliently recover if they can quickly engage in thrilling work rather than the menial tasks inherent in today's job search methodology.

If you have never needed someone messing with your head, protect yourself in your temporarily weakened jobless state. You are an accomplished executive who deals with major challenges and setbacks every day. Why start needing help now. I am very protective of some psychological counselor suggesting flaws in one my clients as a cause of their job loss. In my experience, psychological counseling is one of the major sources of damage in reviewing executive clients coming out of a traditional job search process.

Remember, in biological terms, the loss of a job is just a system correction. That system could be the employer, the executive, the industry, or the markets. You will come to know that these corrections are neutral and foreseeable by watching the signposts of the maximizing machinery.

Any *'mistakes'* that seem to have been made by the executive are simply neutral reflections of the need for a system correction. It could be that s/he needs to find a better context for continuing their biologically maximized career. It could be that they made the leap to a wider expansion of impact, talent, and power around their greatest strengths and they need a bigger context that reflects their bigger system. Again, the correction is neutral.

In the biologically maximized career, your de-hiring is a neutral information feedback event for moving to your next level of operation. If you were-de-hired, there were likely many signposts in reality of a pending system correction. As you learn these signposts, you will be able to proactively take action in the future to capitalize on the correction or to prevent or minimize negative or damaging events resulting from it. This will make a commitment to serial job replacement not only possible, not only profitable, not only strategic, not only adaptive, but also safe.

I invite you to proceed to the next job search article to see a comparison of the old and new job search paradigms and protocols.

27

PROACTIVE SERIAL JOB REPLACEMENT

A career game-changer

A BREAKTHROUGH, HIGH-SPEED, HIGH-GROWTH, HIGH-IMPACT CAREER STRATEGY

The inefficiencies of today's job search protocol may leave the majority of executive job searchers jobless for 1 to 2 years. If we can dramatically shorten that time and remove the challenges, risks, dangers, and damages of the current process, then a powerful new career strategy will become possible.

If we had a high-speed, high-growth, high-impact job search protocol, an accelerated career strategy of serial job replacement™ would be viable. Serial job replacement™ offers tremendous opportunities for growth, wealth creation, and impact across your career.

For example, a wealth-creation strategy based on serial severance packages and signing bonuses becomes possible. Each new job may be negotiated at a higher salary level than the scale in which you are currently imprisoned might allow. Each new job offers new learning opportunities. Further, if serial job replacement proficiency exists, it becomes less risky to take time off between jobs to grow, pursue fields of interests, raise proficiency, and raise earning potential before negotiating your next position.

For those developing new fields, you could take a break to scale new frontiers before locking into a more lucrative or resource-plenty job context which recognizes your upgraded capabilities or new inventions. As luck would have it, the new biologically maximized career strategy that we have been investigating has safe *serial job replacement*™ built into it. Context changes are integral to the normal system corrections inherent in the perpetual maximizing of systems of living systems.

In the last article we reviewed some of the challenges and weaknesses of today's job search protocol. This article will provide a brief overview of a revolutionary replacement protocol. The key improvements will be highlighted. Many of the inadequacies of today disappear with a single paradigm shift. Future articles will provide practical tactics, strategies, and understanding to facilitate using the new paradigm for your job search or indeed any project you want to accelerate and enhance with the power, direction, and capabilities of the maximizing machinery.

ACCELERATED MULTI-SYSTEM JOB SEARCH

Most job search protocols assume that you are a separate biological entity. What if you changed that paradigm? How would job search transform if you instead exploited the fact that you are integrated with all living systems in synergy and synchronization?

How would it change if you could conscript the capabilities of surrounding systems as well as nature's machinery of mechanisms, processes, power, forces, and information that keep all biological systems maximized for survival? Where would your career take you if you rejoined the massive orchestration of all biological systems to maximization and evolution?

We have all seen this maximizing '*machinery*' in action. It keeps our internal organs and systems maximized. Externally, it maximizes systems of systems such as biological ecosystems, stock markets, and economic and sociological systems. How could we harness this maximizing machinery to expedite and elevate your search for that profoundly gratifying, life-enhancing job?

Executives, by definition, spend their days maximizing systems of systems within their companies and markets. By and large, they do it in exactly the same way that nature does. So, let's take a closer look at how you might apply this expertise to capitalize on systems of biological systems.

But before we do, let me first forewarn you that this will not be a tweak here and there to today's popularized job search protocol. This will be a complete re-write. A paradigm shift. This will be a revolution that will spill over into how you achieve goals in every aspect of your life. If you are a fan of today's job search, you may not want to read further. These strategies cannot work in a paradigm based on biological separation.

The magic happens only when one complies with the systems maximizing mechanisms that have evolved the human race. Biological mechanisms, processes, and resources not accessible in any other state suddenly become available to you – both internally and externally – when you operate in your maximized state. In fact, internal and external mechanisms link up. Circuits complete as they have evolved together to do.

It is well worth packaging your goals in such a way as to garner the support of this maximizing flow because that support is significant. The machinery provides the power, the right direction, the right information at the right time, and an abundance of leaps to catapult you ahead. These leaps vary from information coincidences externally to internal leaps to sudden knowledge, sudden creativity, flashes of genius, and whole-brain *savantism*. Included also are leaps to our peak-performance, peak-growth *flow* states: our maximized state.

28

BIOLOGICALLY MAXIMIZED JOB SEARCH

In previous articles, we have been examining the biologically maximized career strategy observable in the lives of such notables as the seven iconic founders of Google, Amazon, Microsoft, Apple, and Facebook. We want to now build on what you have learned to create a biologically maximized job search protocol.

Let's see if we cannot replace the hit-and-miss, meaningless, menial, devaluing, and demeaning tasks of today's job search with a revolutionary approach that is exhilarating, accelerated, nourishing, growth-inciting, targeted, and acutely accurate in its selection of your ideal job.

Today's job search is externally driven. It is about selling yourself into the *available* jobs. In contrast, the maximizing machinery is dedicated to maximizing your biological predisposition. It is internally or biologically driven. Biology pressures us to stretch to apply our strongest talents to creations at increasingly more challenging and impactful levels. We have evolved addictive drives that biologically bias us to use and improve our strongest strengths to maximize. The more you comply with these addictive drives, the more you will want to comply with them.

We are therefore, as expected, biologically biased to growth and peak performance because it is advantageous to the survival of the species. We want to line up our job search strategy and indeed any goal with the direction of this biological bias and predisposition. Therefore, in shifting to a biologically maximized job search, you will be shifting from externally driven selling to internally driven growth. The new protocol will immediately launch you into a high-growth state from day one.

This is what we observed in the careers of our seven super-achievers, Bill Gates, the two Steves, Jobs and Wozniak, Mark Zuckerberg, Larry Page, Sergey Brin, and Jeff Bezos. Their careers were defined by their biologically driven growth path. Their jobs emerged as the ideal next context for that growth to occur.

The jobs emerged as the leaps noted above that are characteristic of partnering with the maximizing machinery: coincidences, sudden knowledge, and flashes of genius. Their unprecedented jobs were biologically created as part of the fundamental creative dynamic of the maximizing process: the re-combining of existing information systems to create new systems.

Alternatively, their jobs were *collided with* by their growth causing them to be re-grouped with more synergistic systems as part of the self-organizing of the larger system of which they were a part. An employer, a partner, a customer – these are just biological systems with which it is logical to group you for synergy. Selling against biological self-organization is unlikely to be successful. It is smarter to go with the flow.

With the biological commitment to growth and maximization, new functionality will emerge during job search or indeed any time you want to harness the maximizing machinery to achieve goals. The very meta-skills needed at executive levels are the ones that develop when biologically maximized. These include improvements to your conceptual, abstract, and big-picture thinking skills, your pattern recognition skills, your creativity, your abilities to deal with ambiguities and unknowns, your expanded consciousness, and more.

You will come out of the job search process with more functionality to bring to your next job. This is in sharp contrast to today's job search which tends to deplete people because they are doing administrative work that they do not like. Today's job search further undermines most by keeping you from using you career or work talents for one to two years.

All of the indicators of operating at your maximum tracked for the twelve categories of past events for the *Sourcing Your Savant* exercises are telling you how to proceed at full speed to your next job. In addition, the *Sourcing Your Savant* exercises enabled you to identify the kinds of work that maximizing has supported in your past. You therefore already have the means to choose goals to garner predictable support in the future.

The exercises give you a glimpse of a dynamic order that you can harness in the future to improve your chances of achieving any goal. They significantly reduce the challenges and risk associated with job search. Trauma and damage will reduce if you know the safe supported direction.

A you would expect, all 12 categories point you into the same direction. Therefore, your ideal job will be indicated, for example, by an intersection of your past-event themes of addictive drives drawing you to pursue certain fields of knowledge, creation, frontiers, and/ or unpaid work. Therefore, you already have the means to adjust your job search process and the job you seek to be able to perform at your maximum to complete a job search in record time.

Positive emotions, passions, and facilitating events will arise as indicators that you are moving in the right direction. Opposition events will emerge when you are off-path. The more you have been on-path, the 'louder' the messages will be when you slip off it. They will be an indicator of the body's rebellion after having experienced the way it was supposed to operate. We know that your growth path is not linear. You now have the means to limit the negatives and toxicity often inherent in today's protocol by moving with the maximizing flow rather than against it.

THE MAJOR DIFFERENCES BETWEEN TODAY'S JOB SEARCH and TOMORROW'S BIOLOGICALLY MAXIMIZED JOB SEARCH

Key job search upgrades when BioMaxed

1. Shift from operating as a separate biological entity to operating as part of a high-growth *system of systems*
2. Major improvements in information sources:
    *   Shift from stockpiling people (networking) as off-chance information sources to sourcing the right information at the right time via the maximizing machinery
    *   Shift to serial information leaps inherent in the maximizing process such as coincidences, breakthroughs, sudden knowledge, sudden creativity, and flashes of genius
    *   Shift to merging with the information sourcing and information creation process that is the essence of the maximizing process
3. Shift from linear to nonlinear job search
4. Shift from the devolution of career skills due to non-use during job search to high-speed growth:
5. Shift from just you alone to multi-system achieving to accelerate your job search success
6. Shift from relying on just your capabilities to those of the maximizing machinery and all of the systems it synergizes and synchronizes thus allowing you to achieve beyond your potential
7. Shift from a job search limited by your intelligence to one directed by nature's intelligence
8. Shift from haphazard progression to a biologically directed job search

9. Shift from externally driven by networking and available jobs to internally or biologically driven to do the work you were meant to do.

10. Shift from having to discipline and push yourself to the necessary unpleasant job-search tasks to being pulled by your additive drives to do work that you love

11. Shift from depleting, menial, job-search tasks to meaningful, nourishing, energizing, growth tasks

12. Shift from applying your weakest skills to job search to applying your strongest ones. Shift from job searching from your minimum to operating at your maximum using your strongest most rewarding talents.

13. Shift from a focus on selling to a focus on growth, amplification, and maximization.

1. Shift from operating as a separate biological entity to operating as part of a high-growth system of systems

The revolutionary job search protocol I am proposing entails a paradigm shift from the job searcher operating as a separate biological entity to one in which s/he is integrated within and capitalizing upon a system of systems. It is about driving a biological machinery which operates in predictable, knowable ways to ensure the survival of the majority of living systems.

Multi-System Achieving

This machinery or systems of systems is relentless in trying to maximize you through synergy and synchronization with the other living systems it orchestrates. Therefore, you have a choice. *You can comply with it and capitalize on it or you can fight it.* Who wants to fight upstream against the flow of living systems seeking survival synergistically? And who wants to be left behind the global trends of synchronized living systems? How much easier it is to mesh your goals with those of the maximizing process in order to conscript its power and magic.

The *Sourcing your Savant* exercises give you insight into your system's maximum and the kinds of goals the machinery has supported in your past and therefore will support in your future. Job search will become fast, easy, and fun when you know how to avoid times where you will not be successful and to increase the times that you will experience success.

If you want to harness the power, capabilities, direction, synergies, synchronization, and information of the maximizing machinery and all of the living systems it orchestrates to support any personal goal, you have only to help it achieve its goals. You need to be continuously striving to operate at your maximum to align your goals with its goals. Your career, your job search process, and the job you pursue will all need to align with pressure to maximize your system.

You will also need to recognize that there are other systems relevant to these goals which are also being maximized simultaneously. The ideal job choice is one in which the employer system provides the best context for your continual expansions while your system is symbiotically pivotal to the expansions and maximizations of the employer system. The maximizing machinery will promote this synergy among systems. It will automatically group systems as part of maximizing the larger system of which you and an employer are both a part. When you merge with the maximizing process you will be pressured to collide with each other through coincidences and leaps. This will accelerate and enhance the attainment of any goal.

We will therefore want to get it working for your job search process. That is why the first task after firing is to create work which stretches you to operate at your maximum using your strongest most rewarding talents hopefully in the service of your job search or salary replacement. This may be the exact opposite of what must happen with today's job search protocol where you are pressured to begin chasing available jobs.

However, from the high-growth state of maximization, it becomes easy to read signposts as to the pathway to desired jobs or even the correct fit of jobs that are offered. It will be valuable to be blocked by impediments when you are selling yourself into a job contrary to the biological goals and predispositions of your system. No one wants a job in which they must continually swim upstream against the current for their system. No one wants to fight their biology. Therefore, finessing a sales pitch to get a job contrary to your biological predisposition will either fail immediately or in the short term.

This is not personal. It is neutral systems maximization. It is about what is best for the survival of all interacting systems in this system of systems of which you are a part. The employer's system, the interviewer's system, the market system, and your family system may all be relevant. When you merge with your right configuration of systems for synergy and synchronization, there will be a tell-tale pattern of facilitating signposts or indicators that will confirm you have got it right.

Multi-system achieving is the fundamental paradigm shift which differentiates the new revolutionary protocol for job search. Merging with the maximizing machinery will not only ensure you are operating at peak performance to conduct your job search. You are likely to even be able to perform and achieve beyond your potential as your capabilities and information are extended by those of surrounding systems.

2. Major improvements in information sources:

- Shift from stockpiling people (networking) as off-chance information sources to sourcing the right information at the right time via the maximizing machinery
- Shift to serial information leaps inherent in the maximizing process such as coincidences, breakthroughs, sudden knowledge, sudden creativity, and flashes of genius
- Shift to merging with the information sourcing and information creation process that is the essence of the maximizing process

One of the most dramatic differences between today's job search and the proposed multi-systems approach is the sources of information that each uses. Networking is the number one strategy promoted for today's executive job search. This entails the stockpiling of people on the off-chance that they may be able to either tell you about job opportunities or facilitate introductions for closing a job. I have discussed this at length in the previous article.

Through partnering with the maximizing process, the proposed protocol provides information in the three ways noted above. If this indeed proves to be true, 80% of the activity of today's executive job search protocol will be eliminated. If networking has not been working for you, now there is an alternative for you to test out.

Breakthrough Synthesis - the new job search / job creation process

It takes a lot of work to source and sustain a network. The returns on your efforts are low and by no means guaranteed. Partnering with the maximizing process offers job seekers the opportunity to source the right information at the right time with very little effort. Maximizing is really just the process of coming up with creative solutions to improve and adapt systems. This creativity emerges from the *re-combining of existing information systems to create new information systems* that are the solutions to maximizing challenges.

I have called this process *breakthrough synthesis* since leaps or breakthroughs are generated. It occurs because the larger system of which we are a part groups systems such as us for synergies, resource-sharing and information-sharing. It orders systems in the same way any CEO would organize company resources. If we comply with its direction, we will be grouped with the ideal systems for leaps to accelerate our job search or indeed any goal we have aligned with it.

The new job search protocol is therefore partnering with an information sourcing and creation process. The existing information pieces that will serve as fuel are borrowed from various systems which have been grouped around us for synergies. Picture this happening as a zipper closing in front of you.

As you move behind the zipper where the borrowed information systems are being re-combined, you will see a dramatic increase in the leaps or new information systems that are its products. Therefore, you have only to line up your job search goal with this zipper and you will be catapulted to your goal by these coincidences and leaps. Move your job search to either side of the maximizing zipper and the number of leaps will decrease.

These leaps or new information-system 'products' emerge from the 'zipper link-ups' as coincidences, flashes of genius, sudden knowledge, and sudden creativity. The leaps even include shifts into our peak-performance, peak-growth states. These are the leaps into the altered consciousness of *flow* states, especially those that emerge from using and improving our strongest, most rewarding, talents on meaningful goals that stretch and challenge them. This is our maximum state so of course it is the goal state pressured by the maximizing machinery.

High-Speed Job Search due to improved information

When you can increase the coincidences helping you to find your job from one or two per month to 20 to 50 per month, you will understand how quickly and efficiently you can locate your next ideal job on your career maximization growth path. This is a far superior ROI than anything pure networking may help you with. Further, these leaps are nonlinear. You may be able to bypass hundreds of linear steps with one information leap. This is another point of comparison of the current and proposed job search process. Let's investigate nonlinearity separately below.

3. Shift from LINEAR to NONLINEAR JOB SEARCH

Nature has figured out that nonlinear is faster, safer, more creative, and more serendipitous with a multitude of coincidences and leaps catapulting you forward. As the next section indicates, even growth is nonlinear. To operate in partnership with biology, then, you will obviously have to unlearn some cultural things such as requiring goal achievement or growth to be a step-by-step linear progression.

The information leaps of which I have been speaking may bypass hundreds of linear steps to speed you to your goal. They may lead to outcomes which may not be possible to achieve linearly. And they may even lead to outcomes or ways of achieving your goals which never occurred to you.

These outcomes may not even be a linear extension of your start point. Rather they may be the product of the process of emergence that is inherent in chaos and catastrophe theory. This may be better understood by thinking of the popularized *butterfly effect*: the sensitive dependence on initial conditions in which a small change at one place in a deterministic nonlinear system may result in large differences in a later state. Would it not be wonderful to have this process working for your job search?

The nonlinear leaps that are the byproducts of the maximizing process are able to take you from one stable state to the next thus minimizing damage or trauma to your system. These leaps and nonlinearity offer unexpected corrections to issues with today's job search process which I identified in the previous article. Job search will suddenly become efficient, exciting, accelerated and, frankly, FUN.

4. Shift from the devolution of career skills due to non-use during job search to high-speed growth:

Even one's growth path, when partnering with the maximizing process, will be nonlinear. The application of your strongest talents to challenges that stretch them will always be central to you operating at your maximum. Therefore, growth will constantly be an amplification, an expansion, an intensification of those strongest talents and their impact on reality. It is not about a linear progression to a new form but leaps to magnifications of existing strengths or predisposition. Expansions of your essence. Your core.

This is why I believe serial job replacement will and should become integral to any career strategy. The more time you spend merged with the maximizing machinery, the faster these expansion leaps occur. After each one you are likely to want to either re-define your current job or replace it to allow you to continue to stretch to your next frontier of capability. There is no smarter career or life strategy than to be paid to grow at maximum speed along the path you would pursue anyway given every resource and freedom.

This is what we observed in the careers of the seven iconic founders of Google, Apple, Microsoft, Facebook, and Amazon. Each lived a biologically maximized career. Their jobs emerged from their advance through new frontiers of their natural growth paths – even if they had to invent unprecedented jobs to accommodate their growth. Their careers were not determined externally by what jobs were available but internally based on successive frontiers of expansions that they were biologically pulled to pursue.

Because they were moving behind the maximizing zipper, the jobs usually found them as leaps created by the breakthrough synthesis that is the maximization process. This is certainly a lot less work than today's job search process and makes the desired *Serial Job Replacement* career strategy entirely accessible. This is no doubt music to the ears of any down-trodden job searcher frustrated by the networking approach.

The maximizing machinery itself may initiate this serial job replacement even without you having thought of it. As the information structure of your system is transformed by a growth expansion, the larger system in which you are housed will group your system with more appropriate systems which have synergy with your newly expanded system. Nature organizes systems as efficiently as a good CEO would do. Synergistic systems and especially those which share resources or purpose are grouped together into 'departments.'

While there are new skills with each growth expansion, there are a multitude of meta-skills which emerge through other aspects of the maximizing process. Expect to dramatically grow your functionality and especially your executive-level meta-skills during your brief vacation from employment. In contrast, today's job search is more likely to devolve you than grow you since you will likely spend 1 to 2 years away from work involving your professional specialization.

Whether you want to launch your biologically maximized career, your job search, or to achieve any goal, you will want to immediately re-center onto your natural core and begin operating at your biological maximum. This is the way to harness the power, the direction, the capabilities, the information, the leaps, and the magic of the maximizing process that enhances and orchestrates all living systems for survival. This process will begin in the next article which offers several start scenarios to suit a variety of career situations.

29

RESET TO YOUR MAXIMUM TO OUTPERFORM YOUR POTENTIAL

O ur cultures have taught us to operate as separate biological entities. This would unfortunately limit our potential to what is within us. Yet, we have been born into a massive biological machinery. Systems of mechanisms, processes, and forces have evolved to adapt and maximize all living systems for survival. Could our potential be extended by that machinery and all the systems it orchestrates? Indeed it can. Change the way we operate and the bar for human potential will be raised.

Let's start by resetting you to your maximum and extended potential. Use the strategies, targets, tactics, and scenario suggestions here to reinstate your partnership with the adapting, maximizing machinery that evolved us all. Once re-connected, our true power, potency, and promise are released. Circuits complete. Processes partner. Mechanisms mesh. Systems synergize and synchronize. Synchronicities surge. Coincidences cluster. Sudden knowledge, sudden creativity and flashes of genius flood in. Growth processes launch. Our internal-external human system resurrects.

Once re-connected, natural mechanisms inside and outside of you will pull you to peak performance and beyond. Let's begin by identifying methods and scenarios which will trigger adaptive processes to restore you to your true maximum. Let's empower you with the ability to achieve beyond your potential. Let's discover the magnitude of the lifetime legacy with which you might advance our world.

STRATEGY

The strategy for this exercise to reset you to your maximum will be simple: Find a context such as the scenarios suggested below to abruptly quantum leap to operating at your maximum with the least risk to your existing way of life. Shift from your limited internal potential as a separate biological entity to your true potential when extended by the maximizing machinery and all of the living systems it orchestrates.

You do not need to be operating at your maximum to couple with the maximizing machinery. You only need to be moving in its same direction towards your maximization. When your speed and direction are right, it will feel as if two gears have re-engaged. The surge in power and potential will be palpable. Once connected, natural mechanisms and processes will take over. Nature knows what to do. Internal and external mechanisms will re-link. The natural integrity of your system will be restored. You will be able to outperform your internal potential.

TARGETS

Natural maximizing mechanisms will re-engage

We have evolved addictive drives that biologically bias us to use and improve our greatest strengths. It is advantageous to the survival of the species that we be biologically biased to peak performance. The more you comply with the addictive drives we have evolved for it, the more you will want to comply with them. Therefore, we need only put you into a scenario in which you begin operating at your maximum and natural mechanisms will work to sustain you at that maximum.

The indicators of operating at your maximum will increase
Merging with the maximizing machinery will increase your experience of the following:

- Serial top-talent *flow* states
- Facilitating events
- Emotional highs
- Events in which you operate at full power
- Your impact on the world
- Your advance of it through creativity and creation
- *Savant-like* Information leaps inside or outside of you:
  - serial coincidences and other facilitators that speed/enhance your progress
  - serial breakthroughs:
    - "*Aha!*" and "*Eureka!*" events, flashes of genius, epiphanies
    - sudden knowledge, sudden insight, intuitive leaps, enlightenment
    - sudden creativity, sudden creation, creative inspirations
- leaps to emotional highs
- *Savant-like* performance leaps and achieving beyond your norm
- Scaling of new frontiers
- Bringing the new into existence
- Serendipitous projects accelerated as if by magic
- Activities which are addictive and difficult to resist
- Activities that are intrinsically rewarding
- The pull of addictive drives pulling you to use and improve your strongest talents
- The pull of addictive drives pulling you to top-talent *flow* states
- The pull of your knowledge-pursuit, creation-pursuit, frontier-pursuit, and core-expansion drives
- The clarity of the pathway of your maximum path of lifetime impact

Progressions similar to live models of the target maximums will be evident

Real life examples help to identify what we are expecting to happen once you reset to your maximum in your selected scenario. Previous articles have examined the careers of seven icons - Bill Gates, the two Steves, Jobs and Wozniak, Mark Zuckerberg, Larry Page, Sergey Brin, and Jeff Bezos, the founders of Microsoft, Apple, Facebook, Google, and Amazon, respectively. They are examples of biologically maximized careers based on addictive drives to using and improving the greatest talents of each. Their careers are peppered with world-changing breakthroughs reflective of savant states that emerge from synchronizing with the maximizing machinery.

We learned how the compliance of these seven icons to biological maximizing processes caused them to lead addictive careers of serial breakthroughs, serial frontiering™ or scaling of new frontiers, serial growth, serial creations, serial emotional highs, and serial *flow* states. Even a few such breakthroughs have made careers life-changing and world-changing. What could your career become with serial breakthroughs and sudden-knowledge leaps such as flashes of genius, "Aha!" and "Eureka!" events, sudden insights, sudden knowledge, sudden creativity, creative inspirations, intuitive leaps, epiphanies, and enlightenment. Even those of ordinary intelligence may cultivate such *savantism*?

TACTICS

Increase Top-Talent Flow

We have determined the strategy and the targets of our reset exercise. It is now time to talk implementation. Your absolute maximum is a peak performance *flow* state that emerges while you are applying your strongest most gratifying talents to your most meaningful goals benefiting the audience most valuing of your efforts. If, in the scenario you choose for your reset, you did nothing but spend your day in this *top-talent flow state*, you would merge with the maximizing machinery effortlessly. Magically, new functionality and capabilities would emerge. Serial achievements beyond your potential would become the norm.

Increasing the time you spend in top-talent *flow* daily is both a target and a tactic. It is, in fact, the one tactic that will eliminate the need for all of the rest of the below prescribed actions for resetting to your maximum. It is a way to turn the task over to natural maximizing processes and mechanisms. This is because *flow* is yet another addictive drive: the more you experience it, the more you want to experience it. This is why it has been a key driver or, perhaps more accurately, attractor of human evolution.

Magic happens when you stretch your best talents to more impactful achievements over long periods of time. You repeatedly experience an altered state of consciousness that psychologist Csikszentmihalyi calls flow. Attention is 100% focused on the activity at hand. Peak performance and growth are built in. Time, space, and even self-awareness cease to exist. Flow is intrinsically rewarding. It too is an addictive drive that will raise your baseline functionality as it did with our super-seven.

Top-talent *flow* will be the ultimate goal for any of the scenarios below that you might choose to facilitate your reset to your maximum. However, should this maximum state elude you, there are alternative approaches which will enable you to re-engage with the maximizing machinery that evolved us. Again, you do not need to be operating at your maximum for your system to merge with the maximizing machinery. *You only need to be moving in the same direction* towards *maximization*.

Honor your savant formula based on your historical experience.

Harness future predictability from past patterns

You may easily know your target maximum state for this exercise from an inventory of your experiences of your maximum in your past. Your Sourcing-Your-Savant exercise findings provide you with the formula for when the maximizing machinery has and has not supported your progress in your past and hence when it will and will not support you in the future.

This formula defines when coincidences, breakthroughs, flashes of genius, sudden knowledge, sudden creativity, and other such flow events will catapult you to peak performance in your selected scenario. Therefore, your savant formula will tell you precisely the design requirements for a scenario for reconnecting you to the maximizing machinery.

Best savant exercises for scenario selection

There are certain themes or patterns of past events that are likely to be the most advantageous for selecting and operating in your ideal scenario for resetting to your maximum. For most people, these include: your unpaid-work theme and your knowledge-pursuit, creation-pursuit, and frontier-pursuit themes. And, of course, your top-talent flow theme will be invaluable since that is the target state we want to increase in any scenario you choose. There is no point in trying to work against what you find in your historical data. Choose your scenario accordingly.

Advance in the direction of increased indicators of operating at your maximum

The very capabilities that you expect to have at your maximum are not just the targets. They are also the tell-tale signs to follow moment-by-moment to arrive at this maximum. They tell you that you are moving in the right direction. Follow the indicators of your maximum state and you will automatically be re-integrated into the maximizing machinery and taken to your maximum in one seamless process.

The criteria used to identify past events of operating at your maximum for the _Sourcing-Your-Savant_ analyses, are the same signals that you will be following to guide you within the scenario you. When these signposts are not in evidence, you will need to take safe actions in any direction until you find them again. You might have _zigged_ when the maximizing machinery _zagged_.

Your new modus operandi: Follow your savant formula and indicators of your maximum

You may recall that this is the thrust of the section entitled: _Why you want to Learn All Twelve Categories:_

"There is an important reason why you will eventually want to investigate all twelve categories. This is because this will not be a one-time exercise. It will become your new routine modus operandi. You will analyze immediate events as they happen to choose the direction that will keep you hugging the flow of the maximizing process. Repeating the exercise for more current events will be the way you will read, merge into, and capitalize on the maximizing machinery going forward. These twelve analyses will provide the information that you need for your daily decision-making, goal-setting, and goal achievement."

If we are resetting you to your maximum, then operating in this way will become your new way of life. You will always want to be directed by the signals of the maximizing machinery. There would be little point to resetting to your maximum if it was not your intent to sustain that maximum. Now you know how to do that. You are ready to make the paradigm shift.

Participate in proactive breakthrough synthesis

Let me offer a little more insight into your new modus operandi. You will be partnering with a nonlinear opportunistic maximizing machinery that is synchronizing and synergizing all living systems for survival and adaptation. The creativity it uses to resolve maximizing challenges is something I have coined '*breakthrough synthesis*' in previous articles.

Breakthrough synthesis is the perpetual process of re-combining existing information systems to create a new information system. Serial breakthrough synthesis is the recognizable serial quantum leap process which underlies all biological evolution. It is what generates the leaps I often speak of such as coincidences externally and leaps internally such as breakthroughs, flashes of genius, sudden savantism, sudden knowledge, sudden creativity, and sudden flow states.

This is the process you are merging with when you reclaim your membership in a massive biological machinery. One goal is to tap into the breakthroughs to accelerate your progress to your goals. However, there is also an opportunity for you to drive this breakthrough synthesis to achieve larger more innovative goals faster. Future articles will help you to develop this expertise.

For the purpose of this paradigm shift or quantum leap to your maximum, it is worth imagining that it will take you three to seven coincidences in order to have the information pieces to recombine into a new information system that enables you to achieve your goal. You will want to be vigilant in letting yourself be guided by the machinery to colliding with the necessary information pieces. Try not to force yourself to proceed linearly through a known project plan. Let yourself become nonlinear and opportunistic wherever it is safely possible to experiment.

Even non-creatives and those with less than stellar intelligence will see how to re-combine three to seven information pieces for breakthroughs when they are placed in front of them. History is riddled with examples. It is possible for you to become one of them. Create what has never existed before. Create your equivalent version of a Google, Facebook, or Apple.

As you spend time in your new scenario, growth processes are launched that will continue to raise your baseline performance and functionality for the rest of your life. In effect, even the information system that is 'you' will become an ingredient in breakthrough synthesis. Even you will be recombined with other information systems to create a new 'you' around the innate immutable essence that is you.

It is important to understand that there is no finite arrival at your maximum. Once your partnership with the maximizing machinery extends your potential externally your potential becomes as infinite as nature. Given this new breakthrough modus operandi, true human potential is as yet unquantified.

Additional miscellaneous tactics for the reset-to-your-maximum exercise

Some additional rules of engagement will ensure the success of your foray into a scenario for your reset to your maximum:

1. Your work in your chosen scenario must impact or advance reality or the outside world in some way.
2. Any action you take should elicit indicators that you are moving towards maximization: a. top-talent *flow*   b. emotional highs   c. coincidences, leaps, and facilitating events
3. Comply with the historical evidence: Pursue those directions and elements that the machinery supports. Exclude the things it has not historically supported.

4. As a novice, avoid emotionally-charged goals until your expertise and proficiency improve. For many this will mean you should not set goals for money, valuing, acceptance and inclusion to compensate for abandonment and exclusion, and abundance to compensate for scarcity.

5. Protect your system integrity at all costs. Where possible, take safe experimental actions only. There is no need to take risks to re-integrate into the maximizing machinery. Risks should be considered 'blocks' to routes you were considering. Keep the same end-goal but find another route or a better time when the machinery is more receptive.

6. Watch for facilitating events or gates to open up to show you the best direction in which to proceed. You should thrill to the prospect of your next action or do not take it. There should be coincidences, leaps and flow events to facilitate your progress in the adaptive direction for you. Alternatively, if there are blocks, even internal ones such as negative emotions, stop. Find a better route to your goal which appears to be supported by the machinery. Nothing should need force.

7. However, never leave a flow event or coincidence unexplored. These are created by opportunities for synergy with other living systems. Take safe actions to find those opportunities. They indicate the adaptive direction for your system.

8. Keep non-play elements to a minimum. Honor *your* goal if you must choose between *your* goal and the goal of your scenario – a charity, for example. It is important not to be pulled off-track. You may already have that situation at work so your scenario needs to be a safe free environment where you can meet your maximizing goals.

9. It is okay to take action with the signposts of the maximizing flow without knowing precisely what your goal is. An

emotional blueprint or how your arrival at a goal will *feel* is sufficient.

30

RESET SCENARIOS FOR THE <u>EMPLOYED</u>

to reset to their maximum by achieving sustained or serial top-talent *flow*

These scenarios suggest contexts conducive to releasing you to reintegrate with nature's adaptation machinery. Once you begin moving in the direction of your maximum, there will come a point of critical mass. Nature will take over and begin pulling you to your maximum and into adaptive directions. Nature's maximizing machinery will begin grouping your system to advantage for synergies and synchronizing. For those who are employed, it is still possible to free yourself to reset to your maximum. Where possible, however, you should keep risks to your current employment status to a minimum until your expertise develops.

Scenario 1:   Redesign your existing job

If employed, your ideal method to reset to your maximum is to re-design your existing job to comply with your natural growth path and the direction the maximizing machinery has historically pressured your system to progress. If this cannot be done directly, perhaps the following strategies might be used:

- Add special projects to your job, especially skunkworks or new ventures. Top-talent *flow* can only be experienced if you are advancing through new challenges and creations.
- Join projects elsewhere within your employer
- Partner with companies that do business with your employer or create projects around the interface

- Create charitable ventures for your employer's corporate giving program which require your strongest talents
- Seek secondments to governments or companies/organizations surrounding your employer which will benefit both sides and you.

Scenario 2: Take a different job within your current employer that already exists
Scenario 3: Create a new job within your employer
Scenario 4: Create a new project or new venture within your current employer

Ideally these will become part of your existing job as part of the job redesign sought in Scenario 1. However, if necessary, work outside of your job on perhaps initially unsanctioned projects until they have advanced enough to be supported by your employer and become part of your job or create a new job ideal for you.

Scenario 5: Take an active Board of Director position with an outside company

This will let you do the work you were designed to do without leaving your employer.

Scenario 6: Work for a charity or not-for-profit after work
Ideally this could be a role sponsored by your current employer as part of their corporate giving program identified in the redesign of your job in Scenario 1. However, it may be necessary to create a new context conducive to resetting to your maximum which is unrelated to your current job or employer.

Caution: For the goals of this exercise, it is important to not be dragged into work which is not related to resetting your system to its maximum. Unfortunately, one must recognize that the needs of the have-nots in this world are infinite. You are taking on this additional work to reset to your maximum in a meaningful way. It is best to restrict the gift you are prepared to give to the giving of your strongest talents applied to your most rewarding and valued work at your maximum. This benefits both sides of the equation while energizing rather than depleting you. The resulting partnership with the maximizing machinery will reposition you to a more adaptive context long-term.

Scenario 7: Cultivate a hobby outside of work in which you can maximize

There is the possibility that breakthrough synthesis may find a way for your hobby or home studies to eventually become your source of revenue and ultimately your career. Remember to choose your hobbies to comply with your unpaid work drives, and creation-pursuit, growth-pursuit, frontiering-pursuit, and top-talent *flow* drives. So many fabulous careers have been launched in a home garage.

Scenario 8: Research projects undertaken for your employer

These projects should comply with your knowledge-pursuit, creation-pursuit, and frontiering-pursuit drives. Achieving breakthroughs that will advance your employer or your industry will advance your career, upgrade your worth to your employer, and become the driver of your biologically maximized career. So many phenomenal careers have begun with a single breakthrough.

Scenario 9: Give Speeches. Write books. Blog. Teach. Pursue a field of study

The preparation and delivery of material you are passionate about developing within the territory of your strongest talents will pull you into serial top-talent *flow* states. This will give you access to the magic associated with coupling with the maximizing machinery and its serial breakthrough synthesis. Even a few breakthroughs may be career-changing, life-changing, and even world-changing.

31

RESET SCENARIOS FOR THE <u>UNEMPLOYED</u>

to reset to their maximum by achieving sustained or serial top-talent *flow*

This collection of scenarios for resetting to your maximum capitalizes on the increased flexibility of the unemployed. The scenarios are grouped into two categories:

Scenarios 1-4: This set of contexts for biologically normalizing include *assembling* a company, *buying* a company, *starting* a company, or *borrowing* a company or job

Scenarios 5-7: This second category of scenarios is fashioned directly from the seven iconic founders of Google, Facebook, Microsoft, Apple, and Amazon we have been examining in earlier articles. It is about releasing to your natural drives for growth, creation, frontiering™, and learning until you are able to commercialize them into *paid* play, often with the creation of a new field or frontier. This is the means to achieve your maximum lifetime legacy and really explore the outer limits of your capabilities.

Scenario 1: Assemble a mature virtual company from existing components:
companies, firms, professionals, technology, information systems, contractors, consultants, workforces, skills, and such.

This is one of my favorite techniques for quickly resetting my outplacement clients to their maximum to accelerate their job search process. A virtual organization is assembled to provide the perfect context to replicate one's past maximum events.

It should therefore comply with your findings from your Sourcing-Your-Savant exercise: your unpaid work, creation-pursuit, frontier-pursuit, and core-expansion themes and especially your historical formula for top-talent flow. Anything that does not help you to persist in serial top-talent flow states is outsourced. Anything that is more work than play is outsourced.

Virtual company design

This scenario is not about starting and growing an entrepreneurial company from scratch. This is about melding fully operational units together as a mature company. Nor should this model be used to recreate a lost job. The job was lost due to system corrections which may well have been instigated by the adaptivity needs of your own system. There is little future in trying to go against the flow of the maximizing process.

The maximizing machinery found your de-hiring adaptive for some human system whether that system was yours, the company's, the market's, the industry's, or some other system. There had to be many thwarting signals consistent with no support by the maximizing machinery that you had to overlook to end up experiencing the surprise loss of your job.

Now that you know what to look for, you will not be blindsided again. In the future, you will proactively reposition with the signposts of the maximizing machinery to be led out of the old context and into a new more adaptive one.

Coincidences, breakthroughs, flow events, and quantum leaps will catapult you nonlinearly and opportunistically to endgame jobs or the success of this newly created customized virtual organization. When you have the right design for your system, the virtual company will almost form itself.

There will be magic. There should be lots of leaps propelling your forward. So even if you have only an emotional blueprint of the final company design or how it will feel, you can move at top speed to implement it. Partnering with the maximizing machinery will ensure that your natural growth path will become the company's growth path.

The virtual company is intrinsically rewarding in and of itself. However, it will also be one of the fastest ways to penetrate the *hidden job market* to close your ideal job. This will require a separate article to explain. Suffice it to say that your marketing efforts for selling your virtual company's services will coincide with selling yourself into your ideal job.

Scenario 2: Buy a company with private equity

You may not need to create a virtual organization to reset to your maximum. You may be lucky enough to find a company that will give you your ideal job for operating at your biological maximum and you can simply buy the company. Look for flows to facilitate finding the right company and blocks to the wrong one.

Scenario 3: Start an entrepreneurial company along your natural growth path

The design of the company should offer the perfect expression of the maximum you. The growth path of the company should align with your knowledge-pursuit, creation-pursuit, frontiering-pursuit and core-expansion or growth drives. The goal is to be paid to achieve your maximum lifetime growth and achievement.

Scenario 4: Borrow a company and/or a job

An interim employment contract is a great way to normalize to your maximum. Employment could be at a company, a not-for profit, an association, a charity, or similar. If there are no interim executive jobs available, it may be advantageous to offer your services for free to speed your reset to your maximum. Coincidences and breakthroughs may then quickly catapult you to a more permanent arrangement.

Scenario 5: Free-form work driven by your unleashed top-talent drives: Unpaid-work , and knowledge-pursuit, creation-pursuit, frontiering-pursuit, core-expansion, and top-talent flow drives

This is a completely unstructured approach to freeing your day to the above drives in order to advance the world in some way. This is intrinsically rewarding in and of itself. However, over time you will begin to scale new frontiers in your top-talent territory. A plethora of breakthroughs, coincidences, and leaps will pull you in unknown directions which in 20/20 hindsight will appear immensely logical and adaptive. You will find that your version of Amazon, Google, Microsoft, Facebook, or Apple will emerge.

This is a frontiering adventure into new territory or bringing the new into existence. It is pure serial breakthrough synthesis. Rather than having a defined structure for a project or entrepreneurial company, this is about being pulled by the drives and passions associated with applying one's strongest talents until the field, the job, the invention, the discovery, or the company emerges.

Scenario 6: Analyzing and developing your 'science'

This is not about true science. This is about the development of a set of rules or procedures or discoveries that will allow those without your innate talent to operate as you do or to accomplish goals you were able to accomplish. You are seeing my *science* in these articles. They capture what I do instinctively so that others without my aptitude may apply it to achieve beyond their potential. As you analyze how you use your strongest talents you will be increasing your abilities and breaking through new frontiers. For some, this scenario will allow them to achieve top-talent *flow* states and reset to their maximum. It will work for the employed or unemployed.

Scenario 7: Pursue your lifetime legacy

There are those who know what they want their greatest lifetime legacy to be based on the maximum application of their strongest talents applied to the most worthy cause for the most receptive and valuing audience. By committing to its achievement using the breakthrough synthesis of the maximizing machinery, you will quickly find that you have reset to your maximum.

32

THE NEW CORPORATE MAXIMUMS

Biology – the Competitive Advantage
No One Foresaw

Biological maximization is the next generation of breakthrough competitive advantage for the future corporation. Individual and multi-individual human systems are maximized by nature's adaptation mechanisms in exactly the same way. Therefore, the techniques for biologically maximizing yourself that you have learned in previous essays may be applied to maximize all human systems - an individual, a family, a company, a marketplace, a country, and the human race as a whole, for example.

I nearly wrote the obvious article which extrapolates from individual to corporate maximization. But then it occurred to me that it might be more intriguing for both reader and writer if I assumed that both the employees and the corporation are already maximized. This would give us a view of the goal state of maximized corporate operation. It would reveal the potential company of the future.

We will therefore assume that both individual and company have both already partnered with nature's machinery for adapting and maximizing all living systems for survival. We will assume that they are thus already operating not only at their internal potential but their extended potential.

This means that we will be assuming that they both have extended their innate capabilities and potential to include those of the maximizing machinery externally and all of the systems it orchestrates. What will the future company look like when populated by employees operating beyond their potential?

Snapshot of a maximized individual in action

First, let's quickly review how the biologically maximized individual will be operating. A snapshot of that state can serve as a model for our discussion of the biologically maximized corporation. Peak performance for a human system is the application of one's strongest talents to the context that will most benefit from them. One's greatest strengths then will thus be applied to one's most meaningful and rewarding work for an audience that will value that work the most.

This work must scale new frontiers either for the individual or for advancing reality. It must change the physical world in some way. There is the requirement for creative and learning elements. This is because the entrance fee to attain our maximum state requires us to be stretched beyond our previous performance levels.

It requires that we apply our strongest talents at increasingly more elevated levels. Obviously, as a successful species, we have evolved addictive or motivating drives to pull us to maximum performance and adaptive advance to improve our prospects for survival.

Until this series of articles, our peak performance or maximum state had been called *flow*. I have identified a subset *flow* state which is even more precisely our maximum. I have called it *top-talent flow state* since it emerges as a result of applying one's strongest talents to advance ideal contexts as identified in the above definition of our maximum.

A requirement for entering this enticing *top-talent flow state* is that the activity that invokes this altered state of consciousness must stretch you beyond your previous capabilities. Therefore, growth in skill and impact are built into this state. Every time you enter *flow*, then, your system will be advancing. In *top-talent flow*, you will therefore achieve peak growth and peak performance. We have evolved drives what will always pull us to this maximum. They have evolved to ensure our survival.

Growth to maximum performance then can never be linear. Your core is a constant. Your strengths, your talents, and your essence are a constant. Biological predisposition determines this core. Therefore, mechanisms trying to maximize you will always pressure you to expand around your core strengths. Think of ever-widening concentric circles. Nature will always pressure you to operate in *flow* states which emerge from applying your greatest strengths.

This is why the twelve *Sourcing-Your-Savant* exercises are so critical. They tell you your formula for operating sustainably in your maximum state. They tell you when the machinery has and has not supported you in the past so that you might determine the formula for when it will and will not support you in the future.

Maximized individuals move with the maximizing flow and never against it. Therefore, they live by this formula going forward. They choose all projects or goals to capitalize on the machinery and to avoid problems. Imagine knowing which projects will or will not work before you begin them.

This will mean that the machinery will support them with a plethora of capabilities, facilitations, and leaps that will catapult them to their goals. Externally these leaps include clusters of coincidences relevant to their goals. Internally, these leaps include breakthroughs, flashes of genius, breakthroughs, "Aha!" and "Eureka!" events, flashes of genius, epiphanies, sudden knowledge, sudden insight, intuitive leaps, enlightenment, sudden creativity, sudden creation, creative inspirations, and leaps to emotional highs.

These leaps are the essence of the maximizing process. They are generated by the re-combining of existing information systems to create new information systems. This is the basic creativity used to solve maximizing challenges. It is the essence of adaptation. Obviously, maximized individuals will automatically merge with a machinery that has evolved to maximize us. They can thus achieve bigger goals better and faster with this *extended potential*. They can achieve beyond their potential.

In addition, your performance will increase in another way. You will be merging with the production line that generates adaptive leaps or solutions. Even non-creatives and those of normal intelligence may come up with career-changing if not world-changing breakthroughs through tapping into this powerful process. Imagine what you could accomplish with a lifetime of leaps. No wonder every one of us wants to know our maximizing formula.

CORPORATE BEST PRACTICES REVOLUTIONIZED

One human-develop continuum

The maximizing machinery maximizes all human systems identically. It neutrally applies the same pressures to every human system. This means that there is only one human-development continuum for individual and multi-individual systems. There is a single human-development continuum for every individual system, every company system, every country system, and so on. Because the maximizing machinery is logically integrated, the new standards deriving from a partnership with that machinery will also be integrated and interlinked.

One Development Continuum for all Human Systems

Individual Development	=	Leadership	=	Leadership Development	=	Organizational Development	=	Career/Talent Development

Maximizing mechanisms and forces neutrally pressure all human systems to develop along the same growth continuum. Fragmented corporate best practices are replaced by a single integrated process.

Figure 2   ©1995 Lauren Holmes

Corporate best practices merge into one process

This translates into a single develop continuum or single process for organizational development, leadership development, talent development, change management, and career management, for example. Because leadership development and individual development use the same systems maximization process, leadership development will become a by-product of pursuing one's natural growth path.

The natural drives of the individual will propel personal advancement. Yet they will also inadvertently pull individuals to meet organizational needs for leading and leadership development as a byproduct.

In fact, you will learn that this singular development continuum pressured by the maximizing flow will merge today's fragmented corporate best practices into a single integrated process. Partnering with the maximizing process will simultaneously revolutionize standards for management science, leading, entrepreneuring, frontiering™, innovation, leader creation, leadership development, organizational development, performance improvement, productivity improvement, project management, high-speed growth, change management, talent attraction, talent retention, talent development, career management, recruiting, outplacement, and more. Pursue improvement in one aspect of running a corporate system and the other aspects will upgrade as well.

Maximizing and synchronizing

With every individual linked to the same maximizing machinery, corporate best practices are merged and simplified. Levels of uniformity and unified advance never before achievable within organizations are possible. Leadership responsibilities can be embedded throughout the employee population without the requirement for hierarchy.

Unprecedented opportunities emerge for not only distributed leadership and decision-making, but also for universal core competency upgrades. Mass maximization and mass synchronization are integral to the maximizing mechanisms that have developed over generations. They can be duplicated within corporations by simply tapping into these ongoing processes being orchestrated by the maximizing machinery, the master.

The learning organization

Learning-to-learn programs may be replaced by the agility and adaptivity inherent in the partnership with the maximizing engine. This new formula for creating the learning organization does not stop here. As a successful species, we already have the drives for learning and adaptivity. The study in figure 3 shows that these drives have been deactivated by cultural interferences. The learning organization can be achieved by simply reactivating the drives and functionality we can see in operation in our children before they are pressured to conform to our cultures around the age of five.

Human Drives for creativity, frontiering and adaptivity have been culturally deterred

A NASA test for hiring innovative engineers and scientists
was given to 1,600 children as they aged:

Age group tested	Number tested	Year of testing	Percent in 'highly creative' range
5 year olds	1600 children	1968	98%
10 year olds	1600 children	1978	30%
15 year olds	1600 children	1983	12%
25+ year olds	280,000 adults	1985	2%

George Land & Beth Jarman (Harpercollins, 1992), *Breakpoint and Beyond: Mastering the Future Today.*

Land/Jarman Conclusion: Non-creative behavior is learned. [Yet no program restores our original 98% creativity]
Versus
Frontiering™ Conclusion: We lose 98% of our functionality and potential when culture detaches us from the maximizing machinery inside and outside that evolved us.

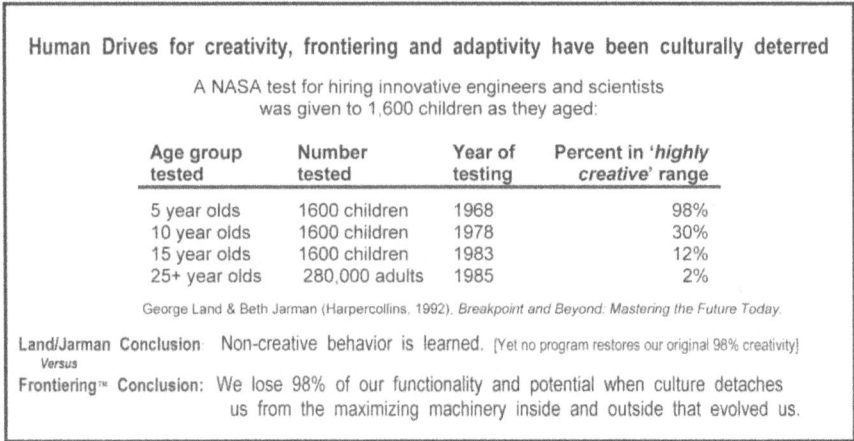

Figure 3   ©1995 Lauren Holmes

Partnering with maximizing mechanisms which have evolved the species will release learning agility from the inside of each employee more quickly and successfully than traditional organizational programs can instruct and pressure learning-to-learn expertise from the outside. The very definition of a learning organization is individuals *en masse* with their drives for learning released.

In addition, partnering with maximizing process makes its themes, modus operandi, and functionality available to us. So, while our own learning, adaptivity, and frontiering drives are being reactivated, we can borrow nature's adaptivity, agility, advance, and problem-solving to operate as if we are already learning experts.

Borrowed creativity and innovativeness

The same is true of organizational creativity and innovativeness. Adaptation is nothing if not a machinery for creativity and creative problem-solving. As above, figure 3 shows that most of us are born creative and adaptive. Our cultures interfere. They provide structured, linear processes which preclude creativity. They make experimentation and the failures inherent in the process risky to our acceptance and advancement.

Because change is feared, those who offer new creative solutions are often criticized and ostracized. Societal mechanisms for resisting change are translated into personal attacks on those promoting change. Funding for innovation is limited to a few fields.

How successful have corporate programs been in making non-creative people creative? Would the success rate not be better if we simply partnered with adaptation's creativity to enable everyone to be creative? And how smart is it that this very process of partnering would reactivate not only the creativity in each of us but the drives that make creative acts addictive? Would our companies not become more competitively creative if we restructured them to free our innate creative drives?

And would that creative competitiveness not be increased dramatically by extending it with the creativity of nature's maximizing process? Of course, it would. Our internal creativity has actually evolved to work in tandem with the creativity outside of us in the maximizing machinery. The synergy enables exponential increases in creativity.

This creativeness inside and outside of us is actually the same maximizing continuum. It was our cultures that decided that our potential and our functionality would be limited to what is inside of us. Our cultures keep us separate from the massive maximizing machinery with which we have evolved to operate at our full *extended potential*. It is our cultures which have hidden our extended potential from us.

It is our cultures that make it unsafe to use the frontiering™ drives which both companies and humanity need to thrive in today's tumultuous world. Imagine the corporate improvements in productivity and innovativeness with the restoration of the full extended potential of each employee. Competitors will be quickly eclipsed. The very capabilities most organizations seek to cultivate through a multitude of corporate programs are accessible through a single shift of every employee to their natural partnered state before culture interfered.

The systems maximizing machinery may be harnessed to maximize your work, to manage your career, and to empower your children to operate at their full potential to achieve their goals. Business leaders may use it to run their companies. National leaders have a new engine for maximizing their countries. World leaders may copy and comply with this multi-system maximizing machinery for running the world differently. We have a new means to adaptively evolve the human race to advantage.

Let's briefly overview a number of additional territories of company operation revolutionized by partnering individual and multi-individual human systems with the maximizing machinery.

33

The New Corporate Maximums
- continued

SYSTEM INTEGRITY HONORED

Individual integrity honored: centered on core strengths

Adaptation maximizes and advances systems synergistically and synchronously for survival. To do this, it honors the integrity of each individual or multi-individual human system. It pressures the integration of each human system around its core strengths and the drives that promote the use of those strengths. It pressures operating from the peak-performance and peak-growth *flow* state that emerges when one is applying these core strengths to advance or be advanced by the contextual system of which it is a component.

This is because the maximization of the contextual system is tied to the maximization and advance of the component system. There must always be synergistic exchanges between them. Our maximum state will always include an exchange. In this *flow* state, only the parts of the brain required for the task at hand are activated. One's body and being move into congruence at the highest performance levels.

This is our most powerful state. This is the strongest configuration of a human system for its survival and adaptivity. This is the state of true integrity of the system. It may not always be possible to operate from this state maximized and centralized state. However, it is understandable why maximizing forces and mechanisms will always pressure us to achieve and sustain this state.

For those who want to extend their capabilities with those of the maximizing machinery, it is important to understand its goals. The closer you are to this centered, self-actualized state, the more you can take advantage of your internal-external system. It is in this state that circuits complete between internal and external maximizing mechanisms and processes. Integrated and centered in this state of integrity, you may most effectively partner with the maximizing machinery for your most powerful and productive state.

Company integrity honored

The above model of honoring the integrity of hierarchic human systems is the same ideal model for peak performance and peak competitiveness of the hierarchic interconnections of human systems around a company: employees, teams, departments, company, the company's business web of suppliers, partners, customers, and support entities.

Competitive breakthrough

Copying evolution's smart model for synchronizing systems into a synergistic multi-system maximization process certainly would add competitive advantage to a company. But here is a new conceptual platform for the real competitive breakthrough: *the powerful maximizing machinery is already driving the company and its associated human systems in this maximizing and synchronizing manner.* Ignore it at your peril.

If a company wants to achieve its goals bigger, better, and faster to outperform and outmaneuver the competition, the maximizing flow is a huge factor. It is both an opportunity and a curse. The direction and biases of the maximizing flow need to be factored in when choosing any goals. If not, there would be a 50:50 chance that your company will end up fighting upstream as it pursues its goals.

The company would have to fight against a large powerful machine. The competitive gap would widen even more if the competitors of this upstream company were flooding downstream with the maximizing flow at high speed while being catapulted ahead by a plethora of leaps such as coincidences, breakthroughs, and facilitating events.

If you want to take advantage of a partnership with all of the powerful mechanisms, forces and capabilities that have evolved to advance human systems, then you will need to honor the integrity of any human system that you are trying to maximize or to conscript to help you to achieve your goals. Now let's see some examples of how corporate best practices will change when we comply with nature's pressures to honor the integrity, growth, and maximization paths of each human system related to the corporation internally and externally.

Growth honors systems integrity

We learned from the snapshot of the maximized individual above that the growth for human systems pressured by the maximizing machinery is not linear. Rather, it honors the integrity of the core strengths of the system. The core configuration remains the same but expands and advances. The key talents and their associated addictive drives advance and become capable of more impact on the context or reality or world.

Therefore, growth, when integrated into the maximizing flow, is an expansion, magnification, and intensification of the 'nucleus' of the human

OUR NATURAL GROWTH PATH AS OUR MAXIMUM CAREER PATH
Excerpted from the video program:
Leadering – Paradigm Shift to
Peak Legacy (Lauren Holmes 2011)
Figure 1

system. Growth is an expansion by concentric spheres. The

configuration of the core of the human system should remain intact. This is what the maximizing machinery is pressuring.

This means that whether you want (a) your company's impact to increase or (b) to use your products to help your customer's system to advance, or (c) to develop your employees, or (d) to increase the contribution of suppliers, the integrity of the core of each human system will need to be honored. If you want to harness the functionality, power, synchronization, synergies, direction, quantum leaps and coincidences of the maximizing machinery, you will need to know where to look for it. You will need to know where the flow is going so that you or your company or your customer or your supplier may move with it.

You will want to select goals to capitalize on an expansion process that already has powerful mechanisms and processes promoting it. You will want to get out of the way as they attempt to expand the capabilities of your human assets or increase the impact of your company.

There are drives within us and mechanisms outside us that can motivate your people to some goals but not to others. With knowledge of the signposts and a little experience, you will be able to quickly identify when the internal and external maximizing machinery is supporting or opposing the directions of your company.

At minimum, you will want to avoid choosing goals that will have you pitted against the maximizing flow. You will not want to promote people up a linear hierarchy which eliminates the use and improvement of their key talents.

Not only will the company no longer have addictive drives motivating the individual's work, it will not have all of the maximizing machinery and the systems it orchestrates supporting the individual. You will not have engaged the extended functionality and potential of his/her internal-external system in the service of corporate goals. You will not have maximized your people.

Now let's examine some examples of how corporate best practices will change when we comply with nature's pressures to honor the integrity of each human system related to the corporation internally and externally.

Customer system integrity honored

Where the maximizing machinery is pressuring a company system to go defines the integrity of the system to be honored. There are multiple systems whose integrity needs to be honored with respect to customers. The more your company, as the supplier company, is providing products or services in compliance with how the maximizing mechanisms are pressuring it, the more successful it will be.

Ideal customers need to offer an opportunity for the supplier company to use their key talents in top-talent *flow* in order to serve that customer. It would go against all of the principles of maximizing human systems to take your company out of *top-talent flow* in order to supply a particular customer. Take a look at the customers that are causing problems, blocks, and negative events. These may indicate opposition by the maximizing machinery. It would not be wise for a supplier company to build its business around these customers.

It is more than likely better to let a customer go than to deviate from the addictive core drives of the corporation trying to take it to its maximum in peak-performing and peak-growth *flow* state. A customer company which requires a supplier company to come off its peak-performance centering will inevitably cost both companies money. A supplier company which is not providing products or services from their zone of peak performance will ultimately both experience and cause problems.

The customer company also has a nucleus of key talents and drives evolved to promote their creative expression. The better your products support the *core creative engine* of the customer company and its expansion around that core, the more successful your company will be as a supplier. The more your products support the directions that the maximizing machinery is pressuring the customer system, the more successful your products will be.

You know what the maximizing machinery is trying to achieve for your company, for the customer company, and for the interface system which develops between the two. Avoid swimming upstream. In addition, if you are setting up a new global company or developing a new product to offer globally, ensure that you also honor the integrity of the global human system and where the maximizing machinery is pressuring it to go.

The goal state of being then would be to support customer companies to move *with* maximizing pressures while your company is also complying with the same maximizing pressures in selecting those products and customers. In other words, both customer and supplier are orchestrated by the same multi-system maximization machinery. They are unified and synchronized externally in the same way that they are unified internally. They are sharing in the coincidences and opportunistic synergies that are characteristic of the multi-system maximizing inherent in a massive biological system of systems committed to the survival of all living systems.

Outsourcing, suppliers, and partners

The same logic which has a company releasing the wrong customers in favor of the right ones, will also dictate an outsourcing strategy which will release suppliers based on the same criteria. A company partnered with the maximizing machinery will spin off those business units that are not part of the company's core competencies and addictive drives. These units will stand out because they will not be acted upon by the maximizing flow in the same way.

While the bulk of the company is enjoying facilitating events and clusters of coincidences, those parts of the company that need to be outsourced are receiving visible opposition from the maximizing flow. Its reaction to a company's components identifies what nature considers part of the system being acted upon. No force-fitting actions by the company to integrate something *non-integratable* are going to make nature change its mind. Its reaction is neutral and final. Proceed against the maximizing flow at your peril.

Having thus *purified* your own company to reflect its core integrity, you will only want suppliers who have done the same. You will not want to choose suppliers to support you with products or services which it really should have outsourced because they are not part of the core competencies of the company. You will want to choose suppliers whose core competency is to provide the product or service which will support your core creative engine.

The same criteria will ideally apply to any partnerships and alliances entered into by your company. Over time, you will gain expertise for quickly identifying the core creative engine of any individual or multi-individual human system. You will be able to quickly have it operating as an extension of the maximizing engine that evolved it. You will be able to quickly re-link the internal-external human system to reclaim its extended potential. You will be able to extrapolate this from learning to maximize and centralize your own system.

Business web integrity honored

The business web of suppliers, customers, and partners that surrounds your company is itself a human system being acted upon by the maximizing machinery. Maximizing your company's business web, then, is as simple as copying and complying with the multi-system maximizing machinery. Do what the maximizing process does and harness its power for you to do it.

Orchestrate systems to co-evolve, co-adapt, synergize, and synchronize the way maximizing mechanisms do. Matrix the capabilities of many systems to enhance company performance. Watch for tell-tale patterns of signposts that your business-web companies are being orchestrated by the maximization process. Then apply multi-system achieving techniques to enable your company to achieve beyond its potential through couplings with co-maximizing companies.

Product development for system unification

System integrity results from the pressure of maximizing mechanisms to unify a human system around its nucleus of greatest strengths and their associated drives. It will be lucrative to choose products which help the maximizing machinery to accomplish this.

For example, the immediate popularity of the Blackberry relates not only to its facilitation of company system integration and unification but also its promotion of the same for the entire system of humanity. The success of technologies which cross cultural boundaries to unify humanity into a single global system will steadily increase over time. This is what the maximizing machinery will always be trying to accomplish. Go with the flow in choosing product and corporate directions.

34

The New Corporate Maximums
- continued

NEW CHANGE MANAGEMENT BEST PRACTICES

We have been dissecting what is going on during the maximizing flow in order to better comply with it and capitalize on it. Let's now look at some examples of how the new corporate core competencies for change management will transform as a result of re-integrating into the maximizing machinery. This machinery serves as the model and the power behind new breakthrough change management methodologies. Many of the change initiatives required today will instead be eliminated by natural levers built into a re-linked internal-external system.

So many of the activities that we consider change management will be included within the daily operations of any company merged into the maximizing process. Maximization is perpetual change. It is nature's adaptation engine. Therefore, natural levers built into our internal-external system will promote ongoing system advance without requiring human intervention.

Overcoming change resistance

Almost all of the resistance to change is fear of the unknown. The methodologies being presented in this essay series are designed to build not only expertise for frontiering™ but a *craving* for it as a way of life. Frontiering™ is the method for penetrating unknown territory or bringing the unknown into existence. It is about scaling new frontiers of knowledge and creation.

By partnering with the greatest machinery for frontiering™ - adaptation or maximization - to remove the fear of frontiering™, our addictive drives for frontiering™ can be released. We become the frontiering beings our successful species has evolved to be.

The effect on organizations of each person having an addiction to frontiering™ and change will be massive. The push for change from employees will replace the pull from management. Fear of the unknown will be supplanted by a craving for living in the frontiering zone. This is the territory where the unknown is replaced by the known, new frontiers are scaled, the unprecedented is the norm, and routine is anathema. This dramatic reversal will revolutionize change management best practices.

By complying with internal and external maximizing pressures, the development of frontiering capabilities will start in one territory of your life and then spread to others. That first territory is around using and improving one's key talents. This is where your internal drives and the pressures of the maximizing machinery are the strongest. We use the pull of the addictive top-talent drives and top-talent *flow* states to mitigate the fear of the unknown associated with frontiering™. There are no negative emotions in top-talent *flow*.

We capitalize on our innate drives to pursue certain passions, frontiers, creations, knowledge, and growth, to build our frontiering addictive drives - or, more accurately, to release drives we are born with as indicated by figure 3. Each frontiering experience will strengthen your addictive frontiering drives. The more you comply with addictive drives, the stronger they get. The more you override addictive drives, the more they atrophy.

Eventually you will have frontiering expertise and frontiering drives which are transferrable to every aspect of your life. The frontiering capabilities that have been culturally deactivated will be reactivated. Resistance to change will decline while the addiction to change increases. This should significantly transform the corporate change management process. Agility and adaptivity will become the norm.

As we partner with the maximizing machinery, we are exposing ourselves to its perpetual change, perpetual adaptivity, perpetual creativity, and perpetual frontiering. Adaptation and maximization are pure frontiering. There is no need for a separate change management competency if both we and our organizations are merged with nature's change management process. We simply choose individual or organizational change goals consistent with the directions that maximization is pressuring and merge with its machinery.

Partnering with the maximizing flow is accomplished, to a great extent, by watching for the patterns of signposts and indicators of its direction. Since the flow is always in a perpetual state of flux, change will become a way of life. However, it will feel as if it is business as usual moment by moment. It will feel safe because one is just following the same signposts. Partnering will provide a dynamic stability no matter how fast the change is occurring.

The fear of the unknown and the resistance to change would return only if a company insisted on a change management program which is in conflict with the maximizing flow. If the company and employees are in sync with the maximizing flow, then there is a powerful engine in place to be harnessed to fuel change projects. The unification and synchronization needed for change management are built into this partnering. Change would be routine. It would become a way of life. This is a significant departure from current best practices.

Quantum leaps for faster, bigger change with reduced risk

Part of the power for organization change management will come from copying, complying with, and capitalizing on the quantum-leap bias of the maximizing flow. A high percentage of organizational change projects derail when they attempt to achieve change through a long linear transition. Invariably organizational systems become unstable. Evolution has solved this. It promotes a nonlinear process of quantum leaps which move systems from one stable state to a new stable state without the risky transitional states.

Because quantum leaps use an emergent process, what happens between the current state and the new state is not known. Quantum leaps are nonlinear because the post-leap state cannot always be predicted from the pre-leap state. The post-leap outcome is not usually a linear extension from the start state. The emergent process mixes, matches, and combines pre-existing pre-leap systems to create new unprecedented post-leap systems. In many cases, the unexpected events and products emerge almost by magic or miracle by this creative process.

A metaphor for the quantum leap process would be to install new stable software on a computer to replace existing stable software. It is transparent to us how the new software makes all of the necessary connections to other software within the computer. If we did not know better, we would think it is magic.

The same re-connections and integrations are happening behind the scenes of coincidences and other leaps such as flashes of genius, breakthroughs, sudden knowledge, sudden creativity, and other such epiphanies. The process is a duplication of the underlying creative process of evolution, maximization, and frontiering: the blending of existing information systems to make new information systems. That is why I call this *breakthrough synthesis*.

A metaphor corporately would be the cutover to a new computer application over a weekend. On Friday you have one application and on Monday you have only the replacement application. To many, there is no more fearful prospect than that Monday experience and the weeks of dread prior to its arrival.

This resistance to change is one of the greatest challenges faced by today's change managers. If all employees become quantum leap experts by partnering with nature's quantum leap process, the challenges of change management would diminish dramatically. Everyone would jump from one stable state to the next without the scary interim steps.

Change accelerated by clusters of coincidences

Best practices for change management will not only be transformed by the self-initiated quantum leaps of the previous section but also by the maximization-initiated quantum leaps that are inherent in any partnership with the maximizing machinery. They include clusters of coincidences and leaps to flow states, sudden knowledge, and spontaneous creativity. They serve to catapult the company ahead nonlinearly to its goals, to better versions of its goals, to goals that cannot be achieved linearly, or to alternative goals which will better serve the company system.

35

The New Corporate Maximums
- continued

NEW PROJECT MANAGEMENT BEST PRACTICES

Project management has developed over the years as a major new form of management in organizations facing rapidly changing business environments. The Project Management Institute (2000) defines it as "the application of knowledge, skills, tools, and techniques to project activities in order to meet project requirements." Project management is intended to provide focus for using resources to achieve a specific objective. The fundamental objective is to "get the job done" to client satisfaction within time, cost, and performance constraints.

Today's project management best practices will appear primitive by comparison to what is possible by merging with the maximizing machinery. Project plans promote a linear process with pre-set steps rather than the opportunism, creativity, adaptivity, and nonlinear quantum leaps of the maximizing flow.

Project plans and processes are limited to *human* knowledge, intelligence, power and capabilities rather than those of maximization. They are *man-run* rather than *nature-run*. They are limited to the capabilities of the human mind.

Projects run with the today's methodology do not garner functionality, resources, or advantage from either the maximizing machinery or from the co-maximizing systems it orchestrates. They do not benefit from opportunistic synergies. Nor are they pulled with the trends of synchronization with the majority of other human systems.

Without this multi-system maximizing process, projects will not be catapulted ahead by the leaps and facilitating events that are its byproducts. There will be no clusters of coincidences, sudden knowledge, sudden creative inspiration, Aha! experiences or models of solutions. In fact, the inability to penetrate unknown territory or to deal with known and unknown unknowns is a weakness of today's project management methodologies that is solved with finesse by the maximizing machinery. Today's projects would also not harness mechanisms that would maximize the project system for peak performance as it does for any human system.

Many unpredictable events happen during a project including opportunities to upgrade the performance of the project. Working to a project plan interferes with working opportunistically and nonlinearly. Rather than following a linear project plan, evolution uses creativity and adaptivity to capitalize on the best options and resources at each decision juncture. The new project management standards will enable each step to be based on the results of the previous step to yield significantly superior results.

Another benefit of partnering with evolution's machinery is that it enables projects to achieve the *intent* of their goals in bigger and better ways than might have been anticipated. The most fundamental dynamic of maximization is breakthrough synthesis: the re-combining of existing information systems to create new information systems to solve maximization, adaptivity, or synchronization challenges. This is the essence of adaptation's creative process. It becomes available to your project with the partnering.

Another beneficial upgrade to best practices then is that partnered project results may dramatically exceed what was originally sought. Consequently, how project goals are defined will need to change to enable the emergence process and adaptation's creativity to step in to create the best possible outcome to meet the intent of the projects and the true needs of a maximized corporate system.

Current project selection does not factor in the maximizing flow. They not only do not benefit from it, but incorrect selection could pit the project against that flow. This will build failure into the project. With the quantum leap process, projects can proceed from one stable state to the next just as evolving living systems do in nature. The need to keep transitional organizational systems stable through a linear process is avoided. Nature was smart enough to figure out that there is danger in the linear approach. Perhaps we could embrace the same learning.

Nature has developed a nonlinear process for achieving breakthroughs for a reason. Evolving the human eye through linear transitional states, for example, is not possible. Similarly, some projects should not be undertaken because there is no way to achieve their goals through the linear process built into today's project methodologies. The proposed new project best practices correct for this.

The new standards for selecting projects will be based on what has historically been successful in all project-related human systems. The *Sourcing-your-Savant* exercises will identify where the maximizing machinery will or will not support the progress of the project and its implementers. Better project selection will ensure better project results. Honoring project system integrity and that of the participating human systems will accelerate progress.

Project teams currently need to be controlled, disciplined, and motivated to project plans. New best practices will capitalize on the addictive drives innate to the individual to *pull* them to perform. They will capitalize on what the maximizing flow identifies as the strongest talents of the individual. *Top-talent flow* states will be promoted. This will promote peak performance and peak addictive pull for project participants. Project teams using the new methodology will outperform what they could do using the old methodology. Less management and less discipline will be required. More passion and more emotional highs will exchange push for pull.

With everyone synched to the maximizing machinery, distributed leadership, creativity, and frontiering become possible. Hierarchy in the teams becomes redundant. The superior functionality of maximizing mechanisms will be available to everyone. The merger will add new *meta*-skills, dynamics, reflexes, and modes of operating. The inherent ability nature's adaptation machinery to improve functionality will ensure more capabilities for project success.

By partnering at least one frontiering expert with the field experts in each project team, projects will have the expertise for penetrating unknown territory or capitalizing on opportunities that emerge during project implementation. It will become part of project management best practices to include one or more frontiering™ experts within each project team. Frontiering™ experts will become a critical team resource for all breakthrough projects or new ventures to supplement experts from the project's field of endeavor. It is easy to envisage a Frontiering™ Office existing as a subset of the Project Management Office (PMO).

36

The New Corporate Maximums
- continued

LEADERSHIP AND LEADERSHIP DEVELOPMENT

Leadership and leadership development will transform significantly and in unexpected ways with the shift to partnering with the maximizing flow. All of the functions performed by a leader are integrated into the multi-system maximization process. Natural leaders copy, comply with, and capitalize on this process. They operate as an extension of it.

The maximizing flow includes ongoing opportunistic synergizing and mass synchronization of co-maximizing systems. This suggests that if individuals pursue a partnership with the maximizing flow, they may end up with the functionality of leaders as a byproduct, even if that is not their intention.

Frontiering™ is the fundamental dynamic of the maximizing machinery. Frontiering™ is also the fundamental dynamic of leadership in the new partnered way of operating. The person with the expertise for penetrating new unknown territory will always be the leader. In fact, as the ability to frontier becomes more wide-spread, frontiering™ will become the defining requirement for leadership. Again, it would seem that leader drives, reflexes, meta-competencies and capabilities may emerge inadvertently from the proposed partnering process.

Could it be that the global leadership shortage will diminish by partnering with the maximizing flow? As one pursues personal gain in a biologically maximized career, will leadership be created and developed as a byproduct? There is only one human development continuum for all human systems when they reintegrate into the maximizing machinery that evolved them. Therefore, the answer is 'yes.' Multi-system maximizing, multi-system achieving, mass synchronization and synergies, and frontiering - all driven by their associated addictive drives - can indeed both create a leader and make a leader effective.

With all employees synched with the maximizing flow, organization-wide distributed leadership and frontiering™ will replace hierarchical leadership. Leadership will become the capability and responsibility of every individual within the organization. Once they know how to maximize their own system by partnering with the maximizing machinery, they will know how to maximize any human system, whether it is the company, a subordinate, a customer, a supplier, a market, an industry, or a project.

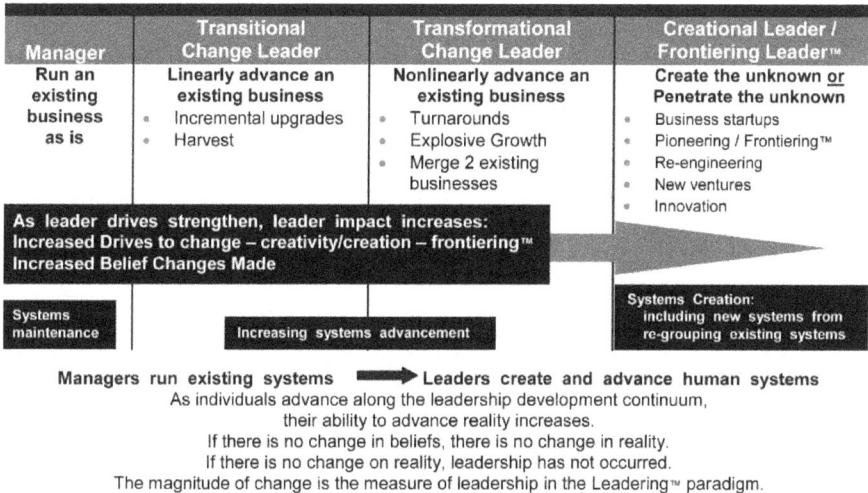

Manager	Transitional Change Leader	Transformational Change Leader	Creational Leader / Frontiering Leader™
Run an existing business as is	Linearly advance an existing business • Incremental upgrades • Harvest	Nonlinearly advance an existing business • Turnarounds • Explosive Growth • Merge 2 existing businesses	Create the unknown or Penetrate the unknown • Business startups • Pioneering / Frontiering™ • Re-engineering • New ventures • Innovation

As leader drives strengthen, leader impact increases: Increased Drives to change – creativity/creation – frontiering™ Increased Belief Changes Made

Systems maintenance | Increasing systems advancement | Systems Creation: including new systems from re-grouping existing systems

Managers run existing systems ➡ Leaders create and advance human systems
As individuals advance along the leadership development continuum, their ability to advance reality increases.
If there is no change in beliefs, there is no change in reality.
If there is no change on reality, leadership has not occurred.
The magnitude of change is the measure of leadership in the Leadering™ paradigm.

Leadership and Frontiering Development Continuum
Figure 4   ©1995 Lauren Holmes

The definition and development of leaders will change with re-integration into a maximizing flow which is adapting, advancing, and frontiering™ continuously. Frontiering™ skill will replace the need for leadership. Managers manage what exists. Leaders bring the new into existence. The resulting leadership development continuum will progress from a manager running an *existing* organization, to a transitional change leader adding *linear* advancement to the organization, to a transformational change leader adding *nonlinear* change to an organization, to those leaders or individuals who have mastered the unknown - *a creational leader* and *a frontiering leader*. These individuals (a) bring the new and unknown into existence or (b) penetrate new or unknown territory respectively (See figure 4).

This is the same skill development continuum that emerges as individuals become frontiering™ experts. The person who knows how to penetrate the unknown will always be the leader. As indicated by figure 4, there is another dimension to this progression.

Systems maintenance, for which no change is made, gives way to increasing *systems advancement* in which linear and nonlinear changes are made. This then progresses to *systems creation* which includes the underlying creating dynamic of maximization and indeed the universe, *breakthrough* synthesis: the creating of new systems by re-combining existing systems or parts thereof.

Everyone who partners with the maximizing machinery will, in effect, become a multi-system achiever in the same way that every leader is. They will achieve bigger goals faster through capitalizing on other systems in the same way that every leader does and the maximizing machinery does.

The biological machinery maximizes human systems. Corporate leaders must maximize human systems. When the two join forces, every best practice for corporate success is revolutionized. Few companies have foreseen the magnitude of this pending transformation to management science. The corporate landscape will be littered with those who fail to make the leap before their competition.

37

COACH-CLIENT CO-EVOLUTION

Have you experienced it?

Many coaches, in their moments of inspiration, have given profound advice to their clients which was exactly the advice they needed for their own lives. I will tell you why I think this happens. I will also hint at how you may selfishly cultivate this handy synergy to accelerate your own problem-solving and growth while giving great coaching.

However, I want to hear from other coaches, mentors, leaders or parents: Have you ever experienced symbiotic growth with your 'coachees' through your own insightful coaching?

My perspective

Here are the why and how hints that I promised. I am a biological anthropologist specializing in career and talent maximization. As such, I am biased towards analyzing how internal and external biological factors influence our nature, behavior, and culture.

I routinely re-integrate clients back into the biological machinery that adapts, evolves, and maximizes us for survival. By extending their capabilities with adaptive biological mechanisms, processes, and systems, clients are able to achieve beyond their potential. They are able to achieve bigger goals better and faster. They are able to penetrate new territories or bring unprecedented creations into existence more quickly, safely, and effectively because that is built into nature's adaptation process.

Exploit nature's self-organizing for synergy and survival

Biological systems self-order for improved survival. Translation: Nature is a good librarian and CEO. It groups all living systems into their most advantageous proximity for information-sharing to solve adaptation challenges. This ordering includes coaches, clients, and solutions. After all, we too are just information systems.

Rather than being separate entities, we are all elements of a single dynamic information matrix or database. This database is really just a single integrated flow of living systems continuously re-ordering and synchronizing for synergy to ensure their mutual survival.

Source the right client at the right time?

Any assumed separation between coach and client then is cultural not biological. The events in either life inform the other when one releases to nature's adaptive self-ordering process. When one complies, one is ushered to the right client at the right time to source the information to adapt or advance both coach and client. Has anyone experienced this?

Client clustering?
Access more coaching insights

As a natural extension then, going with this adaptive flow actually causes a clustering of clients to provide the information required to adapt or maximize the coach's system and each other. Needless to say, this clustering is wonderfully efficient from a business and growth perspective. A coach will be orchestrated to deal with the many sides of a personal growth issue across a multitude of clients if necessary until his/her own system has the information required next to correct, adapt, or advance.

These event patterns provide a wealth of new information to make a coach more effective, more insightful, more inspired, more ingenious. Profound and perhaps life-changing coaching may result.

Your experience?

Now it's your turn. What is your experience of these phenomena or absence thereof? Has seeming serendipity ever crept into your coaching?

38

THE ULTIMATE CAREER STRATEGY

What do the founders of Amazon, Microsoft, Apple, Google and Facebook teach us?

Many aspire to the success of iconic founders, Bill Gates (Microsoft), the two Steves: Jobs and Wozniak (Apple), Mark Zuckerberg (Facebook), Larry Page and Sergey Brin (Google), and Jeff Bezos (Amazon). They have achieved the goals that many pursue in their careers.

Chasing the success formula

Many mistakenly assume that they accumulated their wealth, acclaim, and world-changing breakthroughs by pursuing these rewards directly. Many therefore try to emulate what their career paths "seem" to have been in order to acquire comparable extrinsic rewards. They try to follow the discipline and linear formulas prescribed by so many of today's success gurus. They are at a loss when their incredible hard work does not pay off as it did for our seven super-achievers.

The intrinsically-driven career

That is because the elusive success formula these seven share is not what would-be imitators thought. Rather, it was the serial pursuit of intrinsic rather than extrinsic rewards along a path defined by biological predisposition and preference. An exercise in my *'Sourcing Your Savant'* article will help you to identify your personal formula.

A nonlinear career path

In the interim, let's translate the formula into generic terms that anyone might emulate. Our seven icons applied their strongest most rewarding, most addictive talents to their most meaningful, impactful application for audiences which would value their output the most. They repetitively broke through frontier after frontier of capability, accomplishment, and impact with those talents and this formula.

Their strongest talents are a constant. Therefore, their advance will be a nonlinear expansion in capability and impact around that core. Think widening concentric circles. In other words, they continuously improved on the thing they do best rather than advancing up a linear ladder to more responsibility, for example. Rather than ladder-climbing, our seven founders were simply thrust to the top by the expansion of their greatest strengths into widening circles of impact. Their success was nonlinear.

The biology factor

Yet what I am promoting is not about clichés such as "follow your heart" or "do what you love" or "play to your strengths." When you get your personal formula correct as our super seven did, there are biological consequences. Biological benefits explode exponentially.

We have been identifying a goal state of operating at one's biological maximum around the use, improvement, and strengthening of one's strongest talents. A plethora of biological mechanisms have evolved to pressure us to operate at this biological maximum to ensure the survival of our species. So, when these biological mechanisms kick in, magic happens. An overdrive engages.

Addictive drives and emotions activate to pull you to use your strongest talents. They make what would be work for anyone else into irresistible, compelling, addictive play for you. Discipline and force become unnecessary to achieve long hours of productivity and peak performance. This was the day-to-day life of our seven super-achievers. No wonder they accomplished so much.

Further, one will be merging with nature's creative process. Even non-creatives may suddenly wax creative. The kinds of breakthroughs and flashes of genius experienced by our super-seven increased significantly. One breakthrough may be life-changing, career-making, and even world-changing.

Imagine the lifetime of leaps these seven founders experienced. Even coincidences increase to catapult you ahead because they are part of the same information-leap process. Routine career strategies could never compete with this kind of capability.

In addition, you will spend most of your day in a peak-performance, peak-growth state called flow. Flow is our maximum state. Therefore, mechanisms have evolved to addict us to it. Every time you enter flow when it is focused on the use or improvement of your top talents, your functionality, skill, and knowledge of your craft will increase. The baseline operation of our iconic founders thus increased over their lifetimes.

There is more in this overdrive state. Flow is actually an altered state of consciousness. It will cause your consciousness to expand. You may better see the interconnectedness of things as a result. Your work will improve with this perspective.

But more importantly, your cognitive capabilities will increase: conceptual, abstract, system, and big-picture thinking, for example. Right-brain activity will also increase significantly. Synergy with the left brain that most cultures develop better will be maximized. The result will be whole-brain operation at levels which exceed the sum of the parts. This further increases what you can achieve. Prepare to transcend!

The biologically maximized career

Imagine what would happen after decades of upgrading, performing, and achieving at your biological maximum as our seven founders did. What will your biologically maximized career achieve? What will '*your*' Amazon, Microsoft, Apple, Google or Facebook equivalent look like?

39

FRONTIERING IS THE NEW LEADERSHIP

The person who can 'frontier' will always lead

Most people are fearful of venturing into the unknown. Yet a world of accelerating change is now the norm. We are increasingly bombarded with unknowns. We look to our leaders to buffer us from their assault. We expect our leaders to get us through safely, quickly, efficiently, and painlessly.

The person with the expertise for penetrating the unknown will always be the leader. This will be true whether or not that person has all of the wonderful capabilities promoted by today's leadership pundits. And it will be increasingly true as the unknowns continue to multiply.

WHAT IS FRONTIERING?

Penetrate the unknown and Create the unknown

Frontiering™ is a term I coined to label finesse in scaling new frontiers. It encompasses expertise for quickly, safely, and expertly

(a) penetrating new or unknown territory or

(b) creatively bringing the new or unknown into existence.

Frontiering™ is the drive to fearlessly forge futures in the face of the unknown and the unknowable. Frontiering™ expertise equips us to transcend and triumph over unknowns of every specification.

Frontiering is the new leadership

Frontiering™ will become the new leadership. In fact, I would like to suggest that there will be no leadership without frontiering? As change continues to accelerate to become the status quo, frontiering™ will quickly exceed leadership as the most prized skill. The demand for all of us to take risks, to venturesome, to adapt in the face of novel challenges, and to become opportunistic and innovative will rise. The ability to thrive in and exploit unknown frontiers will become the most sought-after skillset of this millennium:

> *Frontiering acumen will determine competitive advantage. Frontiering will determine the next generation of winners and losers, individually and corporately.*

A 2014 redefinition of leadership

Over the decades of the evolution of the concept of leadership, there have been a plethora of definitions for "leader" and "manager." These past stages of evolution dilute and color today's understandings. Clarity for the target expertise has dissipated. Frontiering expertise provides an easy differentiator.

Managers manage what exists. Leaders bring the new into existence. Managers run existing organizations and territories. Leaders penetrate new territories. Leaders advance, transform, and create new human systems. Leaders lead people into new territories or bring new systems into existence.

If you are simply repeating what was done before, leadership is not required. If there is no change in reality, leadership has not occurred. The magnitude of change in reality is the measure of leadership strength. Therefore, the degree of frontiering is the measure of leadership impact.

The new development continuum

As the below figure indicates, the growth in frontiering expertise defines the development continuum from manager to leader. A leadership development continuum emerges based on the degree of frontiering applied. The frontiering-based leadership development continuum will progress from

1. **a manager** running an existing organization, **to**
2. **a transitional change leader** adding *linear* advancement to the organization, **to**
3. **a transformational change leader** adding *nonlinear* change to an organization, **to**
4. those leaders who have mastered the unknown, either **a creational leader or a frontiering leader** or both.

   Respectively, these individuals either (a) bring the new and unknown into existence or (b) penetrate new or unknown territory.

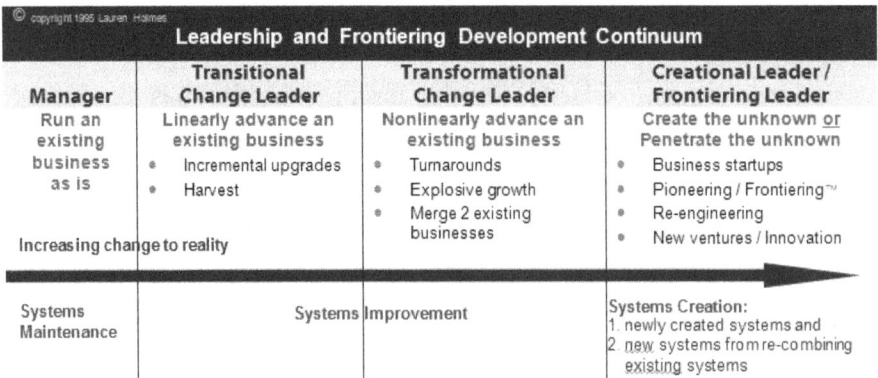

© copyright 1995 Lauren Holmes

Leadership and Frontiering Development Continuum			
Manager	**Transitional Change Leader**	**Transformational Change Leader**	**Creational Leader / Frontiering Leader**
Run an existing business as is	Linearly advance an existing business • Incremental upgrades • Harvest	Nonlinearly advance an existing business • Turnarounds • Explosive growth • Merge 2 existing businesses	Create the unknown <u>or</u> Penetrate the unknown • Business startups • Pioneering / Frontiering™ • Re-engineering • New ventures / Innovation
Increasing change to reality			
Systems Maintenance		Systems Improvement	Systems Creation: 1. newly created systems and 2. new systems from re-combining existing systems

This leadership-skill development continuum is identical to the process for growing individuals into frontiering experts. The definition for leader and frontiering expert is therefore the same. There is no need for leadership if you are standing still.

Secondly, the above continuum also demonstrates another dimension to the progression from manager to leader. Creativity. *Systems maintenance* for which no change is made, gives way to increasing *systems advancement* in which linear then nonlinear changes are made. And finally, one progresses to *systems creation* – usually by re-combining existing systems to create new systems.

Thirdly, as managers advance along the leadership development continuum, their ability to impact and advance reality increases. The ability to change reality is dependent upon the ability to change beliefs. The greater the change in reality required, the greater the commensurate change in follower beliefs that the leader must instill.

Mark the birth of the new definition

I propose we draw a line in the sand to release all past definitions of leader and manager in favor of this 2014 clarity and necessity. The person penetrating the unknown with passion, expertise and, yes, especially addiction, will always be the leader.

Reactivate innate frontiering™

The exciting news is that, as a successful species, human beings are born with frontiering drives and skills. In childhood, we are all in a perpetual state of frontiering to learn everything that we must in order to survive and integrate successfully into a complex and ever-advancing world. Most children experience surprising success in facing, negotiating, mitigating, and surmounting a deluge of unknowns in their first five years of life.

Unfortunately, our cultures and institutions curtail the development of our innate frontiering drives and expertise by pressuring us into more linear and logical modes of operation. Most children begin to find it unsafe to *frontier* once they enter the school system around the age of five. Our cultures make unsafe the trial-and-error required to succeed in new territory, for example. Failure means you *are* a failure, not the frontiering expert who will bring new knowledge, experience, and expertise to the next trial and the next and the next.

Secondly, the pressure to use linear procedures that seldom work in novel situations is another example of cultural interference. The widespread pressure to adhere to linear business plans and project plans are illustrations. Thirdly, sensationalizing media punish rather than support frontiering™ missions which fail. Consequently, millions of dollars must be wasted on making experiments and forays into the unknown guaranteed to be successful before they are begun.

If it were not for the fear of public censure, quick, inexpensive experiments which might fail could accelerate progress. Members of the scientific community are allowed often hundreds of opportunities to fail as they scale new frontiers. The CEO of a publicly-held company may discover that one failure is often his or her last.

As a successful species, mechanisms have evolved which favor and promote frontiering. These include addictive drives pulling us into new territory and creation - the essence of agile adaptivity. *The more you comply with these drives, the more you want to comply in the future.*

Consequently, we need only increase our daily frontiering activity to launch a frontiering way of life. There are biological mechanisms to perpetuate and increase one's addiction to frontiering. Voilà! Both the leadership and innovation shortages are solved in an entirely unprecedented way.

- Could the human race not decide to revise our cultures to free frontiering in everyone?
- What could we accomplish if everyone reactivated the innate frontiering expertise we demonstrated in childhood?

Perhaps this cultural conversion will begin with the pressures of corporate competition. Those companies which choose to make frontiering™ safe for their employees will undoubtedly prevail in the future. Career success will continue to favor those who scale new frontiers. If we examine the most successful careers, it is apparent that frontiering already exceeds leadership as the most sought-after aptitude, expertise, and skillset. Yet they are one and the same:

Leadership for this millennium is defined by frontiering.
Leadership is now, by definition, frontiering.

ABOUT LAUREN HOLMES

All of Lauren's books speak to a new level of human potential possible through a partnership with the biological infrastructure of which we are a part and with which we have co-evolved to operate.

Lauren's education and career were designed to allow her to develop and test her achievement technology based on exploiting this internal-external partnership. She has a biological anthropology degree from the University of Toronto.

Lauren defines how to partner with this bio-infrastructure in her 2001 bestseller *Peak Evolution: Beyond Peak Performance and Peak Experience* and in *BioMaxed* (2019). She introduces a more advanced way to exploit the partnership through the lives of fictional characters in *The Encore: A Transformational Thriller* (2018) as they fight to save the planet.

She then attempts to illustrate the internal-external partnership in action through the lives of real people in *Savanting: Outperforming your Potential*. Here, Lauren retrofits the internal-external partnership onto the well-known lives of some rather successful entrepreneurial CEOs: Bill Gates, Steve Jobs, Jeff Bezos, and Mark Zuckerberg, Oprah, and others.

After first becoming a change leader in global banks, Lauren launched an executive search firm for change leaders for the boards and C-suites of large multinationals. This evolved into providing executive change leaders on contract before that field existed.

Recruiting executives evolved into coaching executives before that field existed. Coaching matured into co-creating new companies, ventures, projects, jobs and frontiers customized to client talents, passions, and strengths to ensure their success. Lauren has been the CEO of Frontiering since 2002. She may be reached through laurenholmes.com or frontiering.com.